MINIATURE GARDEN GROWER

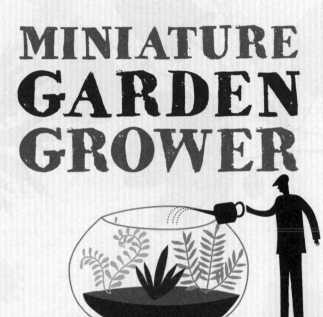

Miniature Garden Grower
Author: Holly Farrell
First published in Great Britain in 2016 by Mitchell Beazley,
an imprint of Octopus Publishing Group Ltd,
Carmelite House, 50 Victoria Embankment, London, EC4Y 0DZ

www.octopusbooks.co.uk   www.octopusbooksusa.com
Distributed in the US by
Hachette Book Group
1290 Avenue of the Americas
4th and 5th Floors
New York, NY 10020

Distributed in Canada by
Canadian Manda Group
664 Annette St.
Toronto, Ontario, Canada M6S 2C8

ISBN: 978 1 78472 171 8

Set in Gill Sans, Madurai and Amatic
Printed and bound in China
Mitchell Beazley Publisher: Alison Starling

Conceived, designed and produced by
Quid Publishing
Part of The Quarto Group
Level 4 Sheridan House
Hove BN3 1DD
England
Cover design: Clare Barber
Designer: Clare Barber
Illustrations: Melvyn Evans
Consultant editor: Simon Maughan

MINIATURE GARDEN GROWER

TERRARIUMS & OTHER TINY GARDENS TO GROW INDOORS & OUT

HOLLY FARRELL

MITCHELL
BEAZLEY

CONTENTS

INTRODUCTION

You don't need a lot of square footage to create beautiful green spaces. Who needs a large garden when you can plant a landscape in a single pot, or an entire ecosystem in a jelly jar? *Miniature Garden Grower* shows you how to create tiny gardens that bring big rewards. With planters ranging from teapots to corks to jelly jars, there are gardens suitable for squeezing into kitchens and bathrooms, living rooms and offices. Outside, a miniature garden can be made simply by adding a pot to the windowsill, the front step or the balcony.

Miniature gardening is not just for those short on space, it's also for those short on time. The gardening projects in this book are easy to create and to look after: no previous experience is necessary. Each planting scheme gives plenty of opportunity for adapting it to your own tastes and imagination.

Injecting a bit of greenery into life has well-documented benefits. These miniature gardens are ideal for inspiring people of all ages to do a bit of gardening, whether it be a windowbox, a pot by the front door, or a terrarium on the windowsill. The chapters are easy to dip into for a rainy (or sunny) day activity, and many of the gardens have the advantage of being instantly complete and mature, making them great gifts for adults and children alike.

HOW TO USE THIS BOOK

All of the miniature gardening projects in this book are easy to achieve, and for many you only need minimal equipment. Each garden is self-contained, and most can be created at any time of year. Dip in and out of the different chapters to create a wide variety of teeny-tiny gardens.

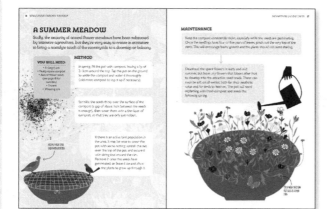

Chapter 1

◀ Miniature landscapes of different habitats are created within a single pot, such as a wildflower meadow or a lush rainforest.

Chapter 2

▶ Terrariums are entire miniature ecosystems contained within glass.

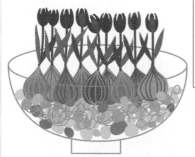

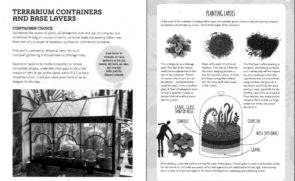

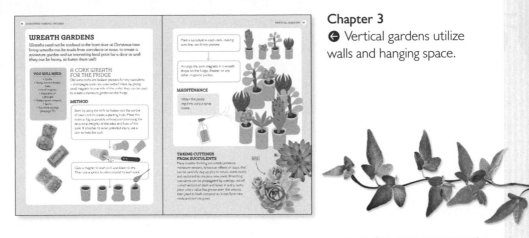

Chapter 3
⬅ Vertical gardens utilize walls and hanging space.

Chapter 4
➡ Water and wildlife gardens show that even the most miniature of spaces can help nature to thrive.

Chapter 5
⬇ Productive gardens enable the growing of a few fruits and vegetables in even the tiniest of spaces.

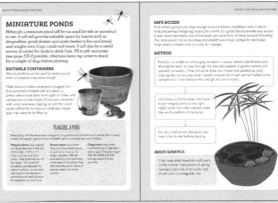

Chapter 6
Specific instructions are clearly laid out in chapters 1–5; for more general advice and definitions of technical terms, refer to Chapter 6: Miniature Gardening Basics (pages 118–137) and Glossary (pages 138–139).

CHAPTER 1

MINIATURE LANDSCAPES

With a bit of imagination and some careful planting, a whole landscape can be created in a single pot. Outside, a woodland of willow trees and spring bulbs, a summer meadow, and a winter forest can all be brought to life. If there is space for all three pots, why not plant them all and rotate them through the prime viewing spot as the seasons change? Inside (or maybe in a sheltered courtyard or on a balcony), you could plant a lush jungle or a terrace of succulents.

A WILLOW WOODLAND

The cycle of deciduous woodlands is mirrored in this miniature landscape of willow trees and spring bulbs. The trees are created from hardwood cuttings, and the bulbs are crocuses.

YOU WILL NEED:

- A (large) pot
- Multipurpose potting soil
- Willow hardwood cuttings
- Crocus bulbs (technically corms)
- Trowel
- Watering can

METHOD

In fall, fill the pot with potting soil, leaving a lip of around ¾in, and tap the base of the pot on the ground to settle the potting soil.

Push in the crocus bulbs (pointy end upwards) to a depth of twice their height, spacing them 2–4in apart.

Water the pot thoroughly (top it up with more potting soil if the level drops significantly).

Insert the willow cuttings, spacing them at least 6in apart. It's best to plant in groups of odd numbers, so depending on the size of the pot there could be 1, 3, 5, 7, or more cuttings creating the woodland.

MAINTENANCE

No chainsaws needed here! Keep the potting soil consistently moist, remove any weeds that appear, and wait for spring. The crocuses' thin, strappy foliage will appear with their little flowers in early spring (get up close to smell their honey fragrance), then the willows will grow new shoots and leaves.

The following year, in late winter, shorten the willows' branches (by how much depends on the available space—judge how much bigger they will get by the growth they put on in the previous year).

CROCUSES WILL ONLY OPEN THEIR FLOWERS IF IT'S SUNNY, WHEN BEES WILL BE AROUND TO POLLINATE THEM

SPRING

SUMMER

WHAT TO PLANT

Crocuses are available in shades of yellow, orange, white, and purple. The spring-flowering (rather than fall-flowering) varieties are a better choice for this scheme. Crocus "bulbs" are actually technically called corms, and are the swollen base of the stem that remains underground. Other plants that have corms include gladioli (*Gladiolus*) and freesias (*Freesia*). For furry silver buds on the willow stems in late winter, common pussy willow (*Salix caprea*) is best, and may be available from florists (trim away the lower 4–6in before taking cuttings as the stem may have dried out too much).

THE PERFECT CYCLE

Deciduous woodlands are very clever ecosystems. While the trees are in leaf, not much light penetrates to the forest floor, and the trees take a lot of the available water and nutrients from the soil, so only the toughest of shade-loving plants can survive. However, plants such as bluebells that do all their annual growing within a short space of time—shooting new leaves and flowering before the trees come into leaf—live in a perfect symbiotic cycle with the trees.

Bluebells live in a perfect symbiotic cycle with woodland trees.

TAKING HARDWOOD CUTTINGS

Trees take many years to grow from seed, but some species are very easy to grow from cuttings. These are pieces of the plant, cut off and placed in a pot of potting soil to grow roots and new shoots, and ultimately to develop into a new plant. By far the most straightforward form of cuttings are hardwood cuttings—small lengths of branches, stuck into the soil in fall or winter, which will start growing as new trees in spring. The easiest trees to grow this way are willows (*Salix* species), although hazels (*Corylus avellana*) and dogwoods (*Cornus* species) are also reasonably reliable.

1 Take cuttings after the leaves have fallen from the tree. Choose a healthy branch about the thickness of a pencil and cut off the end to make a piece about 8in long. Cut just above a bud so that the tree will not be left with an ugly stub of dead branch.

2 Trim the cut end to make a slanting point just below a bud. Insert the pointed end vertically into a pot of moist potting soil. Other than making sure the potting soil remains moist, but not wet, there is now little to do but wait until spring, when the buds above ground should start to grow new shoots. The pot can be left outside, or inside on a cool windowsill.

3 Several cuttings can be taken from the same branch if necessary—just cut as many lengths as needed. Make sure it's obvious which way up they need to go in the pot— it's a good idea to cut the bottom end of each cutting into a point as you take it.

A SUMMER MEADOW

Sadly, the majority of annual flower meadows have been subsumed by intensive agriculture, but they're very easy to create in miniature to bring a nostalgic touch of the countryside to a doorstep or balcony.

YOU WILL NEED:

- A (large) pot
- Multipurpose potting soil
- Annual flower seeds (see page 18 for varieties)
- Trowel
- Watering can

METHOD

In spring, fill the pot with potting soil, leaving a lip of ¾–1⅛in around the top. Tap the pot on the ground to settle the potting soil and water it thoroughly (add more potting soil if necessary).

Sprinkle the seeds thinly over the surface of the potting soil (a gap of about ½in between the seeds is enough), then cover them with a thin layer of potting soil, so that they are only just hidden.

If there is an active bird population in the area, it may be wise to cover the pot with some netting: stretch the net over the top of the pot and secure it with string tied around the rim. Remove it once the seeds have germinated, or leave it on and allow the plants to grow up through it.

PROTECT YOUR SEEDS FROM HUNGRY BIRDS

MAINTENANCE

Keep the potting soil consistently moist, especially while the seeds are germinating. Once the seedlings have four or five pairs of leaves, pinch out the very top of the stem. This will encourage bushy growth and the plants should not need staking.

Deadhead the spent flowers in early and mid summer, but leave any flowers that bloom after that to develop into the attractive seed heads. These can even be left on all winter, both for their aesthetic value and for birds to feed on. The pot will need replanting with fresh potting soil and seeds the following spring.

USE A WIDE SHALLOW POT SUCH AS A BULB PAN

PLANT FILE:
SUMMER MEADOW

It is best to buy seed, rather than taking it from the wild, as then the seed will be guaranteed to be viable (and will therefore germinate), and the seed banks in the countryside will not be depleted. In fact, in some areas it is illegal to take wildflower seeds. If possible, buy native-grown seeds as plants raised in the same climate are more likely to grow well.

Annual wildflowers are available to buy either as single species, or as a mixture of species in one packet (or even a seed "ball"). For a true miniature recreation of an annual cornfield, go for a mix labelled as such, or pick and choose from the plants listed below. Alternatively, use dwarf species to create a miniature field of sunflowers.

Corncockle
(Agrostemma githago)
Magenta-purple flowers and gray-green leaves, reaching up to 30in tall.

Cornflower
(Centaurea cyanus)
The true cornflower has deep blue flowers, but many different varieties are available in shades of purple, pink, white and blue. The thin leaves and stems grow up to 30in tall.

CORNFLOWER

Corn chamomile
(Anthemis arvensis)
White daisy flowers with yellow centers borne on fern-like foliage that grows up to 11¾in high.

Corn marigold
(Chrysanthemum segetum)
Golden yellow daisy flowers and glaucous foliage, reaching up to 20in tall.

Poppy
(Papaver rhoeas)
Very thin stems and leaves bear the scarlet-red flowers at a height of 30in.

Wheat and barley
(Triticum and Hordeum)
Using a few wheat or barley seeds in the meadow will give it an authentic touch, but nigella (*Nigella damascena* 'Miss Jekyll' is a good cultivar) would act as a good substitute—its blue flowers have a meadow feel to them, and the feathery foliage and seedheads are reminiscent of barley seedheads.

Sunflower
(Helianthus annuus)
Good dwarf varieties include 'Big Smile', 'Munchkin', 'Little Dorrit' and 'Yellow Spray'.

Red poppies (*Papaver rhoeas*) are now also known as Flanders poppies from their association with the battlefields of World War One.

A JUNGLE IN A POT

Many jungle species make excellent houseplants: by using several different types it is possible to recreate the layers of plants in a rainforest, from low-growing groundcover to medium-height shrubby plants and climbers or small trees.

YOU WILL NEED:

- A (large) pot
- Multipurpose potting soil
- Jungle plants—at least one for each layer (see page 22)
- Trowel
- Stakes or other supports for climbers, if required
- Watering can

Although this landscape is created in a single pot, this is miniature gardening relative to the scale of the real rainforest, rather than relative to the scale of the room!

METHOD

Decide on where the plants will each be positioned by first of all grouping them together while they are still in their individual pots. Once you are happy with the arrangement, they can be taken out of their pots and planted into the large pot.

Fill the pot around two-thirds full with potting soil, then put in the plants, starting with those with the biggest root balls. Adjust the potting soil level beneath the plants by adding or taking away potting soil as necessary, and filling in around them firmly, so that all the tops of the root balls are level with just under the top of the pot. Water it well and top it up with more potting soil if the level sinks.

Put the pot in a bright room, but not in direct sunlight. A room with some humidity—such as a bathroom—will also be beneficial.

TOP-LEVEL
FLOWERING PLANT

TOP-LEVEL FOLIAGE

MID-LEVEL PLANT

MAINTENANCE

Water the pot regularly—
the potting soil needs to be kept
consistently moist—and feed
with a liquid fertilizer through
the spring and summer.

LOWER-LEVEL
FOLIAGE

Houseplant leaves tend to get coated in dust, so wipe them clean regularly with
a damp cloth. Leaf shine sprays are available that will help keep the leaves clean
and free from limescale spots. Cut out dead leaves and flowers and trim back
any stems that outgrow their space, as necessary.

PLANT FILE:
JUNGLE

Pick tall, medium, and low-growing plants to grow all in one pot to recreate the layers of a rainforest.

Tail flower
(Anthurium andraeanum)
The waxy flowers (usually red) will give some color to the jungle. Mid-level plant (20in tall).

Rattlesnake plant
(Calathea lancifolia)
Also *C. zebrina* and *C. makoyana*. Pale green leaves with darker splotches and prominent, sometimes red, midribs. Lower- to mid-level plant (up to 24in tall).

Dragon plant
(Dracaena fragrans)
Grasslike leaves can reach up to 6½ft tall or more. Mid- to top-level plant.

Rubber plant
(Ficus elastica)
This slow-growing tree has dark green glossy leaves as large as 15¾in long. Top-level plant (8ft tall or more).

Mosaic plant
(Fittonia albivenis Verschaffeltii Group or Argyroneura Group*)*
These plants form a low-growing mat of dark green leaves veined with bright white. Lower-level plant (4–8in tall).

Swiss cheese plant
(Monstera deliciosa)
This gets its common name from the holes in its large leaves. It will need a support to climb up. Cut its shoots back as necessary to keep it to size. Top-level plant (6½ft tall or more).

Heart leaf
(Philodendron scandens)
Large, heart-shaped, dark green leaves are borne on climbing stems. Cut its shoots back as necessary to keep it to size. Top-level plant (6½ft tall or more).

Philodendron
(Philodendron xanadu)
A shrubby, mid-green plant, with attractive leaves on stems that all originate from a central point. Mid-level plant (3¼ft tall).

Bird of paradise
(Strelitzia reginae)
Tall, thin leaves and beautiful pointed orange and purple flowers on tall stems. Mid- to top-level plant (3¼–5ft tall).

RUBBER PLANT

The waxy red tail flower (*Anthurium andraeanum*) is a widely available houseplant.

A WINTER FOREST

Recreating a forest in miniature, by using a selection of trees with complementing colors but different forms, is a stylish way to bring some greenery to a winter windowbox or doorstep. Decorated for Christmas, it's a fun festive project too.

YOU WILL NEED:

- A pot or windowbox
- Multipurpose potting soil
- Dwarf conifer trees
- Trowel
- Watering can
- Decorations (optional)

METHOD

Make sure the trees have been well watered a few hours before planting. Fill the container with potting soil so that the tops of the root balls will be level just below the rim of the container. Tap the base to settle the potting soil.

Take the trees out of their pots and arrange them in the container, considering their relative heights, shapes, and foliage colors. Fill in around the root balls with more potting soil, firming them in well, then water thoroughly. Top up with more potting soil if necessary.

ADD A FEW PINE CONES FOR A FESTIVE TOUCH

MAINTENANCE

Water the forest regularly to keep the potting soil consistently moist, and apply fertilizer through the spring and summer. The container may need rotating to get sunlight to all sides, otherwise the growth will be in the direction of the light and branches in the dark may die off.

Most dwarf conifers are so slow-growing they will not need any pruning, but if necessary trim the branches in spring and/or late summer to keep the trees compact, giving them a very light haircut each time. Either snip off the tips with small shears or scissors to create a smooth conical finish, or cut each branch individually. This takes more time, but the overall effect will be that the trees look more like a natural forest than a manicured topiary garden. Any dead branches should also be removed to encourage healthy growth.

MIX GLAUCOUS FOLIAGE WITH SHADES OF GREEN

BIRDS WILL APPRECIATE EVEN TINY TREES

Individual trees
in pots also make
a good winter display
for a doorstep.

PLANT FILE:
WINTER FOREST

Many of the spreading dwarf conifers are suited to compact gardens, but for a proper forest feel, choose dwarf upright or mounded species. Conifers are naturally slow-growing, taking 20 or more years to reach the maximum height quoted here, so buy in the smallest pot possible (3½in or less) to keep the forest miniature for as long as possible.

Lawson's cypress
(Chamaecyparis lawsoniana 'Minima Aurea')
A miniature version of the conical Lawson's cypress, reaching only 3½ft tall, this has golden, vertical growth.

Juniper
(Juniperus chinensis 'Pyramidalis')
A columnar juniper with gray-green needles, ultimately growing to 3½ft tall.

White spruce
(Picea glauca 'Echiniformis')
A white spruce with gray needle foliage, this forms a rounded shrub 20in tall. 'Jean Dilly' is another variety of this tree that could be used.

Norway spruce
(Picea abies 'Little Gem')
This dwarf Norway spruce has dark green needles and new growth is bright green. It reaches 20in tall.

Black spruce
(Picea mariana 'Nana')
Growing to 20in tall, this dwarf black spruce forms a dense mound of gray-green needles.

Dwarf pine
(Pinus mugo 'Mops')
A dwarf pine with long, dark green needles, it grows into a rounded shrub 3½ft tall. 'Ophir' is another variety of this tree that could be used.

White cedar
(Thuja occidentalis 'Danica')
This dwarf white cedar forms a 20in-tall mound of bright green foliage that flushes bronze in cold weather.

PICEA ABIES

A TERRACE OF SUCCULENTS

Many succulents grow well on cliff faces and on mountainsides, where their inaccessibility helps them to avoid being eaten by hungry (and thirsty) animals. By creating terraces within a broken pot, this environment can be recreated in miniature.

YOU WILL NEED:

- A terracotta pot
- Multipurpose potting soil
- Grit
- Succulent plants
- Trowel
- Watering can

CREATING THE TERRACES

Use a broken pot, ideally with around half of the side completely intact, and the rim around the bottom still together as well. If the pot isn't already broken, a sharp blow with a hammer on one side, about two-thirds of the way up the pot, should do it.

- Mix together enough potting soil and grit, in a 2:1 ratio, to almost fill the pot.
- Fill the base of the pot with potting soil mix.
- Continue to add potting soil, adding layers of the broken pieces of pot to create terraces up the open side.
- Make sure the pieces are securely embedded, and fill around them with potting soil mix to create the maximum possible planting area.

METHOD

Plant the succulents in the pot, using trailing varieties for the front of the terraced space and upright species in the top of the pot. Leave a little space between them for growth, but not too much as they grow slowly and the pot will have more impact if tightly planted.

Water it well. In order to avoid washing potting soil over the edges do it a very little at a time, waiting for the water to soak into the potting soil before adding more.

Cover the exposed potting soil surfaces with more grit. This will reflect light back on to the plants and give a cleaner look to the landscape.

MAINTENANCE

Keep the pot in a sunny, warm place. Most succulents are frost-tender (though do check the plant label), so while they will prefer being outside in the summer, bring the pot under cover (into a greenhouse, conservatory, porch, or on to a sunny windowsill) for fall to spring.

Although succulents are adapted to survive arid conditions, they still need some water, especially when densely planted in a small pot. Water regularly. Many of the green-leaved succulents, such as aloe species, will start to turn red if they are under extreme water stress. If the pot has got that dry, submerge the base of the pot in a bucket or bath of water for several hours, until the potting soil is moist the whole way through again (it may need weighing down initially, so that the bottom of the pot remains under water).

A little fertilizer, diluted to half-strength and applied monthly from spring to late summer, will keep the plants healthy.

Trim away any dead flower stalks and leaves as necessary (you could use tweezers to do this) and clean off dust with a paintbrush or damp cotton bud.

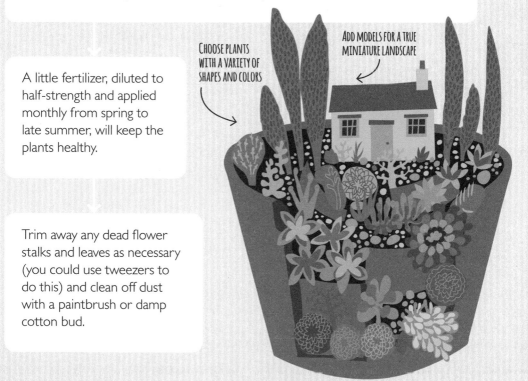

CHOOSE PLANTS WITH A VARIETY OF SHAPES AND COLORS

ADD MODELS FOR A TRUE MINIATURE LANDSCAPE

PLANT FILE:
SUCCULENTS

Although many succulents will bear flowers in the right conditions, it is best to choose varieties based on their foliage and form, as these will be the main display for most of the year. Many are also slow-growing, so even the larger species will be suitable for a miniature garden. In the end it may come down to what species are available, but here are some to look out for:

Aloe
(Aloe)
Generally green, narrow leaves borne in a rosette. Try A. *aristata*, A. *bakeri*, A. *melanacantha*, A. *variegata*, and A. *vera*.

Echeveria
(Echeveria)
Rosettes of pointed leaves, often in glaucous shades. Try E. *derenbergii*, E. *elegans*, and E. *setosa*.

Kalanchoe
(Kalanchoe)
Green or glaucous leaves, often forming new plantlets along their edges that drop off and root where they fall. Try K. *pumila*, K. *millotii*, K. *daigremontiana*, and K. *blossfeldiana*.

Jade plant
(Crassula)
There are many species and cultivars of *Crassula* in a variety of forms. Some look like miniature trees while others resemble coral or other underwater life forms. Look for *Crassula* 'Blue Waves', *Crassula* 'Green Pagoda', and cultivars of *Crassula ovata*.

Sedum
(Sedum)
The classic green-roof plant, many sedums are naturally small and low-growing. Try S. *cauticola*, S. *spathulifolium*, and S. *spathulifolium* 'Purpureum'.

Sempervivum
(Sempervivum)
Their name means "always living;" houseleeks are a popular rock garden plant, too. Try S. *arachnoideum*, S. *ciliosum*, S. *pittonii*, and S. *tectorum*.

ALOE

Succulents have a wide range of forms. Keep leaves shiny by cleaning with a brush or damp Q-tip.

ADAPTING TO THE HEAT:

HOW SUCCULENTS SURVIVE

All plants have evolved certain adaptations not just to live but thrive in their habitats. The leaf could be large, to enable it to absorb as much sunlight as possible in a humid but shady jungle, or small and narrow, to minimize the water loss by evaporation in a sunny, hot climate. Looking at a plant's leaves and other growth habits can tell the gardener a lot about its origins in the wild and therefore where it is likely to grow best in the garden. Plants loosely grouped together under the name "succulents" have all evolved similar characteristics that give them that title.

Some succulents have silvery colored leaves (e.g. *Echeveria*) and stems to better reflect the hot sunlight and therefore minimize their water loss from evaporation.

Succulents come in all shapes and sizes. The largest succulent is the baobab tree—but the tiny lithops species, which resemble small stones, are more suitable for miniature gardens!

In a desert, plants full of water are an attractive proposition for a thirsty animal, so many succulents have defense mechanisms to deter predators. These include bitter-tasting sap and spines on their leaves (e.g. *Aloe*).

All succulents have the ability to store water in their leaves, stems, roots, or a combination of some or all of these parts. They all originate from dry climates, so when water is available the plant takes up as much as it can to use when there is no more water available in the ground, and these water reserves cause the plant to swell up

A LAWN IN A BOX

Beautiful pinstriped lawns can be grown in miniature, too, and there's no need to worry about where to store the lawnmower. Rolls of turf are easy to come by at garden centers and DIY stores, or you could start a lawn from seed. Alternatively, use chamomile plants to create a relaxing, fragrant lawn or seat.

PLANTERS

Lawns do not need a deep planter (a minimum depth of 4in, ideally 6in), but obviously the larger the surface area of the top, the bigger the lawn will be. Boxes are therefore ideal—use wooden wine boxes (ask at a bottle shop), for example, or adapt an old pallet. Drill holes through the bottom for drainage if necessary. Metal tins can be used, with drainage holes drilled in the base, but should not be put in very hot or sunny spots as the metal will transfer the heat to the contents and potentially burn the roots. Really, there is no limit to what can be used to create a lawn, bench or seat.

TURF VERSUS SEED

Laying turf (a pre-grown layer of grass, sold in square-foot strips) gives an instant lawn. For a large area it is relatively more expensive than a box of seed, but may be more economical for miniature gardens, which will use only a few ounces of the seed in a box. However, using seed gives a greater choice of grass species, including mixes suitable for shadier areas, fine lawns, or areas that will get a lot of wear (best for miniature lawns that will be used as a grass seat).

METHOD

Prepare the planter, then fill it with potting soil to within an inch of the top. Water it well.

To lay turf

YOU WILL NEED:
- A planter
- Drill to add drainage holes
- Multipurpose potting soil
- Turf, grass seed, or chamomile plants
- Trowel
- Watering can
- Sharp knife (for turf)

When buying turf, ensure that it is good quality—unroll it to check for weeds and that the grass is healthy and green, and check the soil underside for any pests (see page 132) such as vine weevil. It is common for shops to store turf out in the sun, where it will quickly dry out and die, so make sure the soil is moist. Unroll and water it well once home, and plant it within 24 hours.

Check the planter is full to the correct depth by laying the turf on top and checking the level of the grass: the grass itself should protrude over the top of the planter, but the soil and roots be contained. Top up the potting soil if necessary, then lay the turf piece(s) over the top. Use a knife to cut off most of the excess, then press the turf down firmly. Make sure adjacent pieces are butted up against each other as closely as possible. Again using the knife, cut the turf so it fits neatly within the planter but no potting soil is visible around the edge.

Water it well, and continue to water at least daily until the grass roots have grown down into the new potting soil (test by trying to pull up a corner).

METHOD
To sow grass seed

The box should give an indication of how many ounces are needed per square foot, so work out the area of the top of the planter and divide or multiply the quantity as appropriate and weigh out the seed.

Scatter the seed evenly over the top of the potting soil and rake it in lightly (use a kitchen fork).

Water it to keep the surface consistently moist until the seeds have germinated. Keep birds off the seed by securing some netting over the top of the planter.

To plant chamomile

Space chamomile plants (see page 102) 6in apart (for plants in 3½in pots). Firm the plants in well and water again.

To give the plants time to establish, do not sit on the lawn (if making into a seat) for at least three months, and only minimally for another six months to a year.

MOWING THE LAWN

Miniature lawns call for miniature grass-cutting equipment—a pair of scissors or hand shears would work well. Cut the grass weekly from spring to summer, and brush away the clippings, keeping it to around 1–1½in tall. To get the striped effect, the grass needs to be rolled down in strips, with each strip rolled in the opposite direction. Use a rolling pin, or a glass bottle filled with water, to roll it after cutting.

Chamomile will need trimming only if the plants get straggly (and flowering varieties will need the old flowers cut off regularly).

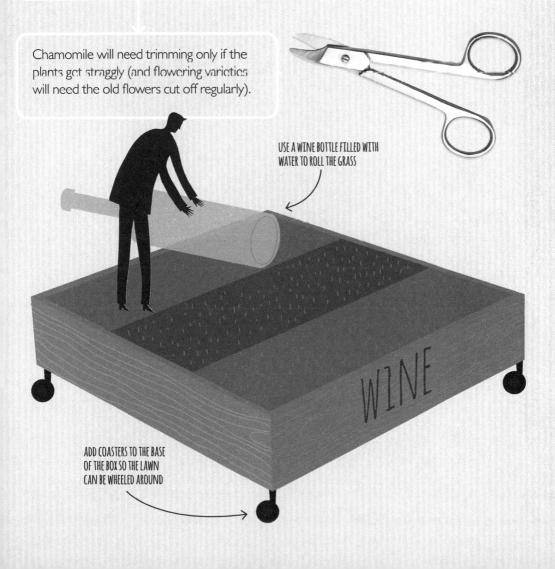

USE A WINE BOTTLE FILLED WITH
WATER TO ROLL THE GRASS

WINE

ADD COASTERS TO THE BASE
OF THE BOX SO THE LAWN
CAN BE WHEELED AROUND

CHAPTER 2

TERRARIUMS

Terrariums are perhaps the ultimate miniature garden: a closed terrarium is an entire ecosystem contained within a vessel that can be as small as a salt shaker. However, open terrariums offer many opportunities to the miniature gardener to bring a wide variety of plants to a windowsill, table, or desk, with no worries about leaking pots. Many different landscapes can be created, from mossy hills to sandy deserts. Alternatively, use a terrarium as a chance to observe a single plant in detail—an orchid, spring bulb, or water lily.

Terrariums are brilliant experiments—especially closed systems—and attractive planters, but don't expect them to last forever when several plants are put in a small container. Ultimately they will outgrow their space, just like any other potted plant, so be prepared to start again if necessary. The original plants needn't be wasted: plant them elsewhere or give them to friends and family.

ECOSYSTEMS IN MINIATURE

Terrariums are ideal to inject some greenery to a workspace or table. Raising the plants closer to eye-level, and planting just one or two within a container, encourages a closer look at just how amazing plants are. Even the less glamorous plants, such as moss and lichen, are no less beautiful when observed in this way.

TERRARIUMS

Terrariums are glass containers for land-based life (as distinct from an aquarium, for water plants and fish). Technically they can contain small animals, too, typically reptiles or amphibians, but plants are lower maintenance. Popular in recent years as an alternative means of displaying houseplants, terrariums date back to the 19th century. They were inspired by Wardian cases, miniature sealed greenhouses created so that plant hunters could safely bring new plants back from their expeditions overseas.

Closed terrariums can survive for many years once sealed. An amateur gardener in the UK created a closed terrarium in 1960, watered it once in 1972, and it is still thriving!

Further proof of the viability of contained mini-ecosystems was gained in 2011, when a scientist lived in a glass box of plants for 48 hours at the Eden Project in Cornwall, UK. No air was added to the sealed room; he was able to survive on the oxygen produced by the plants alone. An interesting experiment, but not one to try at home!

MINIATURE WATER CYCLE

A true terrarium is fully sealed, creating an entire ecosystem within its glass walls. After an initial watering, the plants constantly recycle the water inside so that they don't need any more added moisture.

Water is taken up by the roots and used by the plant for photosynthesis, then expelled through the leaves in a process called transpiration.

In the natural world, the water would evaporate into the air and wider environment, but within the terrarium, the evaporating water has nowhere to go. It condenses on the sides of the container, and runs down back into the soil, from where it is again taken up by the plant for the whole cycle to begin again.

MAINTAINING A BALANCE

A similar process occurs with the air in a terrarium. Plants take in carbon dioxide during the day for photosynthesis, expelling oxygen, then take in oxygen and expel carbon dioxide as they use up the sugars created during photosynthesis. The balance in the air is therefore maintained. Any parts of the plant that die off fall to the base of the plant, where they will rot back into the soil, providing nutrients for the living plant to take up.

TERRARIUM CONTAINERS AND BASE LAYERS

CONTAINER CHOICE

Sometimes the choice of plants will dictate the style and size of container, but sometimes finding an unusual or quirky container leads the planting. Either way, there are only a couple of necessary qualities for a terrarium container.

First, and in contrast to almost all other forms of container gardening, it should have no drainage holes.

Second, it needs to be made completely, or almost completely, of glass, preferably clear glass to allow maximum light to get to the plants within. If it is to be a closed terrarium, it will also need some form of lid or stopper for the top.

Good choices for terrariums are vases, apothecary or jam jars, lanterns, fish bowls, test tubes, and even light bulbs (with the filaments removed).

PLANTING LAYERS

In the base of the container should go three layers of materials: gravel, charcoal, and soil/potting soil. In total they should take up about a third of the height of the container.

First, add gravel as a drainage layer. The size of the stones needs to be appropriate to the size of the container. There's no reason why it can't also be decorative—colored stones could be used, or even crushed glass. A layer of sphagnum moss on top is optional: it helps to prevent the soil washing down into the gravel.

Next, add a layer of activated charcoal. This acts as a filter for the water, keeping bacteria at bay. It's available online, or from pet shops and garden centers (it's the same stuff that's used in fish tanks).

The final layer before planting is potting soil. Potting soil is sterile and will not import any plant pathogens (harmful organisms) that can come from using soil from the ground. A seed-starting mix is best, especially for the smallest containers, as it has the finest texture, but multipurpose potting soil that has had any large lumpy bits sieved out would also be fine.

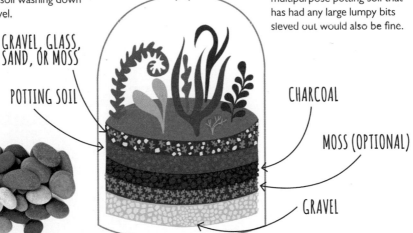

GRAVEL, GLASS, SAND, OR MOSS

POTTING SOIL

CHARCOAL

MOSS (OPTIONAL)

GRAVEL

After planting, cover the surface around the base of the plants. Gravel, glass, or sand is particularly useful for terrariums of cacti and succulents, which will appreciate the additional reflected light. Alternatively, put in a layer of moss (see page 56 for more information on collecting and cultivating moss).

TERRARIUM PLANTING

Before choosing a container, consider whether your choice of plant is practical for a terrarium: remember, everything that goes into the terrarium has to fit through the neck of the vessel. However, there are little tricks to ease the process.

PLANTING TIPS

Use a funnel made from folded paper or card to add the gravel, charcoal, and potting soil. This helps to direct where it is being poured for a neater finish.

Remove as much soil as possible from the plants' roots, and trim long roots if necessary in order to fit the plants through narrow-necked containers and into the potting soil layer.

Kitchen tongs and skewers can be useful for maneuvering plants around in the container, especially those with a narrow neck.

Choose plants appropriate to where you will be putting the container—is it warm, or cool? How much light will it get? Keep terrariums in bright light, but out of direct sunlight, or the plants will scorch. The leaves will still grow toward the brightest natural light source (a process known as phototropism), so rotate the container regularly to maintain even growth.

DECORATIONS

Using objects to decorate a terrarium is a matter of personal taste (and sometimes available space). Natural materials can complement a planting, such as pieces of terracotta, stone, or wood. Decorations can help to interest children in the project, so perhaps add one or two toys, such as tigers or dinosaurs for a jungle effect, or even create a proper tiny fairy garden (search online for suppliers of small-scale furniture and other props).

Why not try some colored gravel?

MAINTENANCE

Open terrariums will need some moisture, especially in a centrally heated room. It is best applied with a spray bottle to avoid overwatering; check the soil's moisture level regularly.

Once sealed, closed terrariums should not need any maintenance other than to clean the outside of the glass. At the first sign of any mold, fungus, or pest infestation, the affected parts should be removed. It may also be necessary to periodically trim back plants that are becoming too large.

FOLIAGE AND FLOWER TERRARIUMS

Many plant species that can live happily without direct sunlight prefer damp conditions to dry, so will therefore thrive contained within glass, in an open or closed terrarium. Generally, these are plants used purely for their (evergreen) foliage, such as ferns, but many other species such as begonias, spruce, and peperomia will also do well.

METHOD

YOU WILL NEED:
- Open-necked vase/jar/fishbowl
- Multipurpose potting soil
- Ferns and/or flowering plants
- Trowel
- Watering can

Plant mini-ferns with mounded or sphagnum moss around the base.

Combine a variety of different species in a single container.

Alternatively, group a collection of different styles of container each planted with the same fern species.

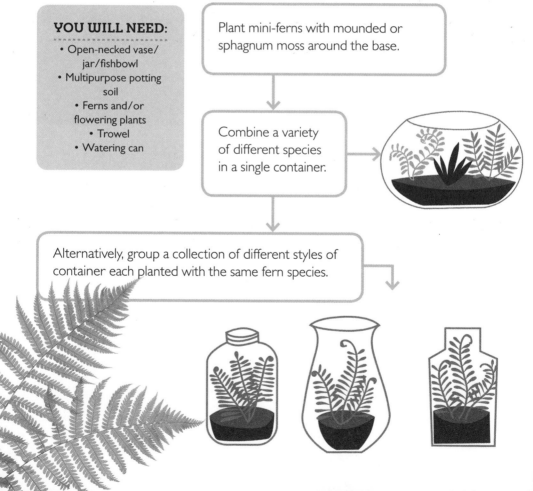

WHAT TO PLANT

Flowering plants are best reserved for open terrariums, because the high humidity in closed containers can cause the delicate flowers to rot. Orchids and African violets (*Saintpaulia*) are two species that do well in a terrarium.

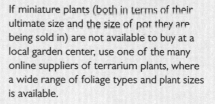

If miniature plants (both in terms of their ultimate size and the size of pot they are being sold in) are not available to buy at a local garden center, use one of the many online suppliers of terrarium plants, where a wide range of foliage types and plant sizes is available.

Phalaenopsis orchids are the best choice of orchid for a terrarium, and the most widely available, including in miniature. Their roots, unlike most plants, contain chlorophyll to aid in making food for the plant by photosynthesis, so they prefer to be exposed to light. Packing the roots into the terrarium with just sphagnum moss and a drainage layer of gravel is the best way to plant them. They could even be left in their original clear plastic pot, which can then be disguised by more moss.

CACTUS TERRARIUMS

Cacti are all succulents, and as such have the same adaptations to the harsh environments they live in: fleshy leaves and stems to store water, spines to deter animals that might like to take a bite out of them. They readily bring to mind a desert landscape, so plant a few in a sandy terrarium.

YOU WILL NEED:
....
- Open-topped glass vase
- Cactus potting soil
- Sand/vermiculite
- Gardening gloves
- Cacti
- Trowel
- Watering can

Use an open terrarium, as cacti will need more light than ferns, and dislike humidity. A wide, open-topped glass vase is the best choice.

METHOD

Cacti require well-drained soil, so use cactus potting soil or mix two parts multipurpose potting soil with one part fine gravel or grit.

Handle the cacti carefully, wearing gardening gloves and holding the pot or root ball where possible. Kitchen tongs around the base of the plant (or an open pair of scissors—don't squeeze too hard) can be used to transfer the plants to the terrarium.

Once the cacti are planted, cover the top of the potting soil with a layer of sand or vermiculite. This will both give the aesthetic effect of a desert and help to reflect light onto the plants.

Place the terrarium in as bright a spot as possible, but not in direct sunlight as the cacti will scorch, and somewhere with good air circulation to avoid the air around the plants becoming too humid.

WHAT TO PLANT

Choose a few different types of cacti to add height and variety to the terrarium. As with succulents, it may come down to availability, but many garden centers stock various species in small pots. Silken pincushion cactus (*Mammillaria bombycina*), glaucous barrel cactus (*Ferocactus glaucescens*), and ball cactus (*Parodia magnifica*) are all relatively small but most cacti are very slow-growing and will take many years to reach a significant size.

MAINTENANCE

A pair of tweezers and nail scissors are useful tools to remove any dead parts or weeds.

Cacti have adapted to take up a lot of water at once (in the rainy season) and then none at all for some time. They will not like to sit in wet soil for prolonged periods. Water the soil carefully, adding a little at a time, until the sand and soil layers are soaked through, stopping as the water starts to drain into the gravel below. Watch the cacti plump up after watering, then gradually dry out again.

SPRING BULB TERRARIUMS

This is not a true terrarium, because there is no growing medium supplied for the bulbs, and because to force spring bulbs to flower earlier, indoors, is a short-term rather than permanent planting. However, growing flowers in this way is fascinating, as it's possible to watch not just the shoots but also the roots develop daily.

YOU WILL NEED:

- A deep glass bowl or vase, wide enough to fit several bulbs (it can also be done with a single bulb in a tall glass)
- Gravel, small pebbles, or crushed glass
- Spring bulbs

METHOD

In fall, fill the bowl or vase about two-thirds full with the gravel and put the bulbs on the top, embedding them slightly so they remain upright. Fill the glass with water so that they sit just above the water level. The bulbs' roots should be able to develop into the water, but the bulbs themselves should not be submerged.

Put the bowl in a cold (cooler than 48°F), dark place (such as the back of the fridge): if the bulbs will periodically be exposed to light, cover the bowl with a paper bag.

Wait until the bulbs have developed plenty of roots and have shoots 1½–2in long. This could take several weeks, so top up the water as necessary during this time.

MAINTENANCE

Move the bowl to a cool, shady spot so that the leaves of the bulbs can turn green. Then put the glass on a bright windowsill in a warm room, away from drafts and heat sources. The bulbs should now start to develop flowers. Continue to top up the water as necessary. Once they have finished flowering, plant the bulbs elsewhere (they won't be suitable for forcing again, as they will have expended too much energy flowering).

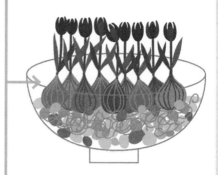

WHAT TO PLANT

Tulips (*Tulipa*), hyacinths (*Hyacinthus*), and daffodils (*Narcissus*) are the best choices for this planting, and are generally all available to buy in small bags or individually at garden centers in fall. It is best to buy ordinary garden bulbs rather than those advertized as "prepared" for forcing, because prepared bulbs may have poor results.

THE SCIENCE

For a bulb to be forced to flower before it ordinarily would, and indoors rather than in the ground, it needs to be tricked into thinking that it has experienced winter outside. It therefore needs to be in the dark and cold before being brought into the warm, at which point it will assume spring has arrived and promptly start growing. This is a process that can also be applied to bring seeds out of their dormancy and is known as stratification.

TOP ⟶

Roots will develop from the basal plate, shoots from the pointed end, so plant the bulbs the right way up!

BOTTOM

CARNIVOROUS PLANT TERRARIUMS

Most plants get their nutrients from the soil, taking them up through the roots. Carnivorous plants evolved in poor soil, and instead get their nutrients by digesting insects that they have trapped in their leaves.

Different species have different methods—the Venus fly trap will snap shut its leafy jaws; pitcher plants have long tubes that unsuspecting insects fall down, into the digestive soup below.

METHOD

YOU WILL NEED:

- Carnivorous plant potting soil
- Trowel
- Watering can

Normal multipurpose potting soil is not suitable. It's possible to buy carnivorous plant potting soils online but they are generally formulated to specific species, so choose your plants first and potting soil second. The plants should be small, but well established. Most nurseries will supply plants in 3½in pots that are at least two years old.

Handle the plants carefully when planting, as their foliage can be delicate. It is also best to leave the surface of the potting soil bare, rather than covering with moss, as the plants are sometimes low-growing (e.g. the fly trap).

Keep the terrarium in a bright, frost-free environment. The plants will be dormant over winter, and can be moved to a less prominent position provided they still have good light and temperatures over 50°F. They can also be moved outside over the summer for a few days (especially if there is a concern they are not catching enough flies), provided they are not in direct sunlight.

MAINTENANCE

Keep the potting soil moist at all times, watering only with rainwater, not tap water, which is too alkaline. A water tank under a drainpipe is the most efficient means of collecting rainwater, and an easy and environmentally friendly way to water any plant. Otherwise, more rainwater will collect in a shallow, wide-topped container than a deep, narrow one.

Remove any dead leaves or flowers as necessary.

The plants will not need any fertilizer.

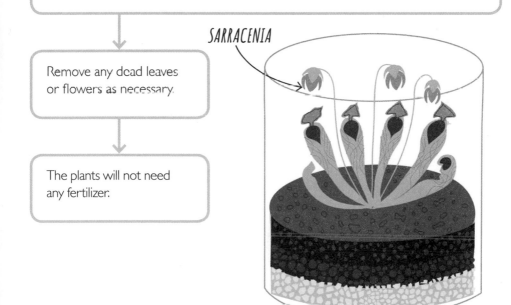

SARRACENIA

WHAT TO PLANT

The various species prefer different soil conditions; choose those that prefer boggy rather than free-draining soil and plant only the same species within a single terrarium. Purchase plants that you can verify have been grown commercially. Never dig up carnivorous plants from the wild. Suitable species include:

- Venus fly trap (*Dionaea muscipula*).
- Sundews (*Drosera capensis* or *D. aliciae*) roll their leaves up around their prey.
- Irish butterwort (*Pinguicula grandiflora*). Its sticky leaves trap gnats and other small flies.
- Pitcher plants (*Sarracenia*). *S. purpurea* has purple pitchers.

AQUARIUMS

Containers of water need not include fish: water plants are just as pretty to look at and by planting one in a glass container, it's possible to see what usually lies unseen, beneath the water's surface.

A large jar or open-necked vase makes a brilliant observation tank for a single water lily, but to keep it going for longer, an oxygenating plant would be a good addition to the water. Make sure the container is at least 12in tall and has a wide enough top to accommodate the leaves and flowers of the water lily.

METHOD

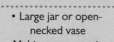

Place the pot in the base of the container and fill around the outside and over the top (carefully) with gravel to disguise it. Slowly fill the container with water, stopping once the stems of the leaves are fully extended and the leaves are sitting on the surface. Carefully separate any tangled leaves if necessary.

If you are using the hair grass, insert it into the gravel in small clumps.

Keep the container in bright but not direct sunlight, in a cool room.

MAINTENANCE

Top up the water level as required.

↓

If the water becomes cloudy, an aquarium/fish tank water cleaner can be used. Check the label to get the correct dosage for the size of the container.

↓

Remove any dead water lily leaves and flowers as necessary, and trim the hair grass if it gets too tall.

WHAT TO PLANT

Small water lilies (Latin name *Nymphaea*) include *Nymphaea odorata* var. *minor* ("*odorata*" means fragrant), *Nymphaea tetragona*, or the pink-flowered *Nymphaea* 'Pygmaea Rubra'. *Nymphaea* 'Pygmaea Helvola' has yellow flowers. Use hair grass (*Eleocharis acicularis*) for an oxygenating plant.

MOSS AND LICHEN TERRARIUMS

Moss and lichen are two of the most remarkable, and yet unremarkable, organisms in the plant world. Lichens, of which there are nearly 2,000 species in the UK alone, grow on other plants (especially tree trunks and branches), wood, stone, and more.

They may be upright, or cling to the surface, but rarely get taller than 2in, making them ideal for a miniature garden. Lichens are actually two or three different organisms living together—a fungus, an algae, and/or a cyanobacteria. The exact state of the symbiotic relationship is open to scientific debate, but it is probably mutually beneficial. They live off the air and each other, not whatever it is on which they are growing. Moss and its amazing traits are featured more on pages 64–7.

Moss likes cool, damp places, such as shady woodlands.

GATHERING MOSS AND LICHEN

When taking moss and lichen (or indeed any plant) from the natural world, there is a code of conduct. Never collect from nature reserves or other protected areas. The moss and lichen types specified for the two terrariums below are not rare or endangered, but only take as much as is needed and no more, and only from places that have large areas covered in moss/lichen so that it can repopulate easily.

The best types of moss for these terrariums are the mound- or cushion-forming species; those that look like mini grassy hills and are often found on roofs, walls, and other stone or brick structures. Using a knife, carefully scrape and lift each mound off the surface, leaving as little behind as possible.

The lichens that grow on tree branches are especially beautiful, and come in a range of glaucous and yellow colors. Rather than scraping the lichen off the branch, cut a section of the branch off entirely (see page 59 for more detail).

PLACEMENT AND MAINTENANCE

The terrariums will need bright, indirect light, but tolerate slightly shadier conditions than most plants. A relatively cool spot, away from heat sources, is best. They will need virtually no maintenance other than to be sprayed with water occasionally—both prefer slightly humid, but clean air, so plant lichens only in open terrariums (in fact, the presence of lichens indicates good air quality). Moss alone will be fine in a closed terrarium.

ROLLING HILLS

This terrarium is a great, low-maintenance way to introduce some greenery to a desk or table. It could also be made into a fun project for children by adding a little toy sheep (make one from some cushion stuffing or plastic—natural fibers will rot in the humid air).

YOU WILL NEED:

- Large jar or open-necked vase
- Multipurpose potting soil
- Gravel
- Moss
- Decorative objects as desired

METHOD

This terrarium could be made with or without a lid. If the stag tree is included (see opposite) it should be left open.

Create the layers of the terrarium as on page 43, then press the moss mounds down on top. To get a larger surface area, try laying the container on its side, and create some peaks and troughs in the potting soil as well to maximize the effect of the hilly landscape.

MAINTENANCE

Water open terrariums regularly using a spray/misting bottle to prevent the moss drying out. Use rainwater if possible.

STAG TREE

Stag trees are those trees in the landscape, typically oaks, which have died and lost their smaller branches, leaving a few large branches that resemble a stag's antlers. Their striking outlines can be created in miniature, with the added benefit of beautiful lichen to observe in miniature.

Find a lichened branch with an interesting shape, small enough to fit into the chosen container. Branches that resemble a miniature tree are best. Alternatively, cut a few smaller lichened twigs and bind them together at the base with invisible thread or fishing wire to form a small tree shape.

YOU WILL NEED:

- A tall glass vase or bottle
- Superglue or gravel
- Invisible thread or fishing line (optional)

The branch(es) will dry out and die, but the lichen, given good growing conditions, will continue to thrive for some time.

No potting soil or growing medium is needed at all, if the branches are put in a container by themselves, so they could just be bedded into some gravel to keep them upright, or stuck to the base with superglue for a truly minimal look.

Alternatively, plant up a moss terrarium as on page 58, and insert lichened branches into the potting soil as tree(s) dotting the landscape.

CHAPTER 3

VERTICAL GARDENS

The most miniature of miniature gardens are the vertical ones. They prove that lack of a garden, or even of a windowsill, is no barrier to growing beautiful plants. Vertical gardens take one of two forms. In the first, the plants are grown in some form of container that is suspended from the ceiling or mounted on the wall. Alternatively, by using plants that do not require a growing medium at all, they can be used to create a picture or mobile.

AIR PLANT MOON

Air plants are ideal candidates for vertical gardening; they live, as their name suggests, off the air alone. Combine a group into a ball and their glaucous foliage creates an indoor living moon.

YOU WILL NEED:

- Chicken wire or similar wire mesh
- Thin lengths of wire (e.g. florists' wire)
- Wire cutters or strong scissors
- Air plants (*Tillandsia usneoides*, also known as Spanish moss, works well)
- Ribbon/string/invisible thread/fishing line

METHOD

Create the structure first by molding the wire mesh into a ball shape—large or small—and securing the edges together with lengths of wire. Trim off any protruding or sharp bits of wire to create as smooth a sphere as possible.

Take one air plant at a time and carefully attach it to the ball using a loop of wire. Make sure the plant is secure, but that the wire is not too tight around the foliage, or it will be strangled. Repeat, so that the whole of the wire ball is covered with foliage and there are no bare spots when it is suspended in the air. Layering the plants slightly helps to keep the foliage cover dense.

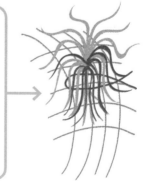

Before attaching the last plant, tie a piece of ribbon to the ball (or use strong invisible thread—a double or triple line—to make it look as if the moon is hovering in the air). Once the ball is fully covered, hang it from the ceiling. Choose a spot in full sun, but not too close to a heater or radiator or it will dry out too fast.

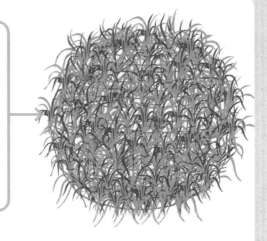

MAINTENANCE

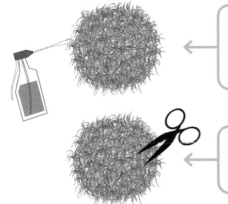

Spray the ball daily with water (rainwater, if possible) using a misting bottle. If the ball dries out, dunk it in a tub of cool water.

If the plants get too straggly, simply trim the foliage with scissors.

LIVING ON AIR

Air plants belong to a group of plants known as epiphytes, which (in the wild) grow on other plants. Unlike, for example, mistletoe, epiphytes only use the plant they are growing on for physical support, and don't take any nutrients or water from their host. Instead, they absorb moisture from the air, and nutrients from dust and other debris that blows over its leaves.

MOSS ART

Moss is another plant that will thrive on virtually nothing. It will also grow back from the tiniest of fragments. Grow different species within an old picture frame to create a living work of art: their varied colors and textures can be combined into abstract forms, landscapes, or even portraits.

Even homes with zero space for growing outside need not look out on to a bare, boring wall: painted with moss "graffiti," it can become a view of rolling hills or trees that is forever green.

See page 57 for information on gathering moss.

YOU WILL NEED:

- Old picture frame, still with the backing but no glass
- Corrugated cardboard
- PVA glue or glue gun
- Paintbrush (for applying PVA glue)
- Moss plants
- Spray bottle

A MOSS PICTURE

For the best effect, use the types of moss that form neat little compact mounds—try to find plenty of different shades of green and/or textures to create the picture. A Mondrian-style works well, or be ambitious and "paint" a portrait or landscape instead!

METHOD

Cut the cardboard to fit the frame and secure it in place with the backing. Decide on the design of the picture, and draw it out on the cardboard as a guide.

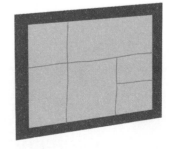

Paint glue onto the cardboard a small area at a time (or use a glue gun).

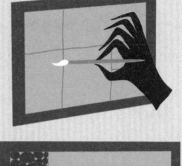

Press the moss on firmly, holding it down for a few seconds so it sticks properly. Repeat until the whole frame is filled. (Take care not to touch hot glue directly: to stick on shaggy moss with a glue gun, press down with more moss than is needed and shake off the excess.)

MAINTENANCE

Hang the picture on the wall. It will need some sunlight, but will cope in a relatively shady area. Avoid placing it near heat sources that could dry out the plants. Spray it daily with water (ideally rainwater), using a misting bottle.

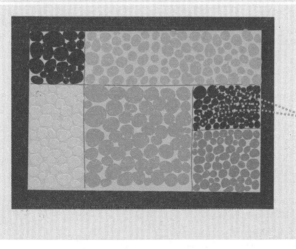

MOSS GRAFFITI

Not many plants would grow back to their normal size having been put through a blender, but moss will survive it and go on to thrive. Take advantage of this remarkable trait to literally paint moss on to a wall. The quantities below are approximate—it's not necessary to be exact when measuring out the ingredients.

METHOD

Wash the moss to remove any soil particles and tear into small clumps. Put the moss, water, water-retaining gel, and buttermilk into the blender and pulse until it reaches a relatively smooth, gel-like consistency.

Pour into the bucket or bowl. The mixture should be grainy but not lumpy.

YOU WILL NEED:
- Moss plants (three cups)
- Water (three cups)
- Water-retaining gel (quarter-cup)
- Buttermilk (quarter-cup)
- Blender
- Bucket or bowl
- Paintbrush

Use the paintbrush to spread the liquid moss on to the wall in your chosen design. You could do it freehand, by using a stencil, or by marking out the lines on the wall in chalk first.

MAINTENANCE

Moss graffiti will do best on a shady wall. In other spots it may need misting with water twice-weekly or more to keep it alive.

The moss will naturally want to grow beyond the design—keep the lines clean by cutting and scraping off the moss with a knife.

KOKEDAMA

This ancient Japanese art means "wrapped in moss."
It has been given a modern update in the Netherlands
to create a hanging garden without any container at all.
Plants are wrapped in a ball of clay-like soil and
surrounded with a layer of moss tied in with string.

YOU WILL NEED:

- A plant
- Peat moss
- Akadama (bonsai soil, available from online retailers)
- Mixing bowl
- Sphagnum moss
- Waxed string or polyester twine
- Grass seed (optional)

The whole thing is then suspended with more string (although they can also be placed on a surface) to create a "string garden." Several plants hung in a group make an interesting miniature garden.

To expand the growing space even further, the moss ball can be seeded with grass or other low-growing plants, although be aware that the grass will only grow upward (see page 72).

Almost any plant can be made into a string garden, although those with large, thin leaves that wilt easily are best avoided, and perennial plants work better than annuals. Choose a hardy plant if it is to be hung outside.

METHOD

Take the plant out of its pot. Fill the pot with two-thirds peat moss and one-third akadama, then tip them both into the bowl and mix thoroughly with enough water to stick it all together.

Crumble the potting soil off the roots of the plant, then mold the peat/akadama soil mix around the roots into a ball.

Wrap the ball with the moss, covering all the soil and pressing it in so it sticks.

Tie in the moss by wrapping it around with the string, trying to keep this to a minimum.

Add another long loop of string for hanging up the ball so that the plant's stem emerges at the top of the ball when suspended. Sprinkle the ball with grass seed, if desired, and hang.

MAINTENANCE

Check if the ball needs watering by weighing it in one hand—the lighter it is, the less water it contains. Water by submerging it for an hour in a bucket of water, then hanging somewhere until it stops dripping before rehanging in its place.

In spring and summer, add liquid fertilizer at half-strength to the water in the bucket.

HANGING GARDENS

If you don't have a windowsill or other surfaces on which to put pots, think vertically. Create the Hanging Gardens of Bathroom, or suspend herb plants over the kitchen table for an easy-reach garnish. Outside, hanging baskets can be a riot of color, or a miniature vegetable patch.

OUTDOOR CONTAINERS

Hanging baskets are readily available. They should be planted densely for the best effect. Wire baskets need lining with a fibrous matting to avoid the potting soil washing out—these are available ready cut. If the bracket will take the weight, why not hang several baskets beneath one another, or create a sphere by wiring two together?

INDOOR CONTAINERS

Specific indoor hanging planters are widely available, from the cheap and cheerful to the seriously stylish, but make sure it is large (or small) enough for the space and its intended plant(s). To avoid muddy drips, it is best that they don't have drainage holes, but if they do, consider where they will hang and whether they can easily be taken down for watering.

With a little bit of creativity and DIY, other containers can be turned into hanging planters as well, such as halved plastic bottles or jelly jars hung with string (try this for a terrarium, see Chapter 2), or put a pot in a vintage birdcage and allow the flowers to come cascading through the sides.

Always consider the ultimate weight of the plant, its pot and potting soil when wet, and the hanging container. Ensure whatever it is suspended with and from are strong enough.

HANGING SPHERE

A hanging basket sphere would be suitable for short-term plants, such as cut-and-come-again salad leaves, but not a perennial planting of herbs. Cut holes in the basket lining to insert young plants, leaving enough space between them to expand, but planting quite densely.

HOLES CAN BE CUT
IN THE BASKET LINING

WHY SOME PLANTS HANG, AND OTHERS WILL NOT

It is possible to buy containers that advertize themselves as suitable for growing herbs and other plants, such as tomatoes, upside down. These are best avoided, because although the plant will hang beneath the pot for a short while, ultimately their hormones will override any gardener's aesthetic intentions and the stems will start to bend and grow upward again. The same is true of non-trailing plants—they will not naturally cascade over the edge of a container.

This is because plant stems contain hormones that enable the plant to grow upward and toward the light, processes known as gravitropism and phototropism respectively. These are essential to the plant to enable it to survive and compete against other plants. It is only many years of breeding, taking advantage of some plant species' tendency to grow prostrate rather than upright, that has resulted in varieties that are trailing.

GRAVITROPISM =
THE TENDENCY OF STEMS TO GROW UPWARD

PHOTOTROPISM =
THE TENDENCY TO GROW TOWARD LIGHT

PLANT FILES:
HANGING GARDENS

Any plant can be suspended in a container, but to get the stems and foliage to hang down over the sides, choose trailing or prostrate varieties such as these:

Annuals
A number of summer bedding plants will trail, such as lobelias, pelargoniums, petunias, and verbenas. Check the label to ensure it is a trailing variety.

Spider plant
(Chlorophytum comosum)
Although the main foliage is grassy and relatively upright, this plant puts out runners with baby plantlets on them that will fall down the sides of the container.

'Silver Falls'
(Dichondra argentea)
The silvery foliage will cascade 3ft or more out of a container. Although often sold as summer bedding, it is actually a perennial and will grow year-round indoors.

Ivy
(Hedera species)
There are many small-leaved ivies suitable for trailing out of containers, indoors or outdoors.

WALL GARDENS

Low-growing and mat-forming plants work best for a wall garden, but they can be annual or perennial.

Salad crops
Try lettuce, cut-and-come-again leaves, radicchio, spinach and chard, pea shoots, and radishes.

Dwarf or tumbling tomato plants
Try 'Red Robin', 'Tumbling Tom', or 'Hundreds and Thousands'.

Annual or low-growing herbs
Try basil, parsley, and thyme, or prostrate rosemary.

Strawberries
These can be grown vertically, too, providing they are well watered. See page 104 for some suggested varieties.

Ornamental plants
Ornamentals good for wall gardens include the mat-forming 'Mind-your-own-business' *(Soleirolia soleirolii)*, *Heuchera* species, whose foliage comes in colors from deep purple to lime green and pale orange, *Sedum* species, and the grassy *Carex* species. *Ajuga* has deep blue flowers, and *Erigeron karvinskianus* will produce masses of tiny pink and white daisies for months over the summer.

WALL GARDENS

A wall garden could be anything from a single plant in a pot on a shelf to a miniature vertical vegetable patch, but all assume next to no space on the ground itself.

GROWING WITHOUT SOIL

Some plants are epiphytic, which means they can collect the water and nutrients they need from the air, but most need to draw up nutrients from the soil. However, advances in technology mean that it is possible to grow ordinary garden plants in no soil at all.

Hydroponics is the name given to this style of growing, and it has two main uses: growing salad vegetables in commercial greenhouses, and green walls or vertical gardens on the side of large buildings. The principle is the same for both: rather than being planted in soil or potting soil, the plants' roots dangle in a continuous flow of water and liquid fertilizers, pumped around from a tank, absorbing what they need but not drowning because the constant movement also aerates the water.

This allows the salad growers to monitor the plants and immediately adjust the nutrient balance in the fertilizer to address any deficiencies in the plants. For a green wall, the weight of the garden is vastly reduced without any soil, and it ensures the plants are all watered and fed, which would otherwise be a rather difficult task.

GREEN WALLS

While many commercial and large-scale green walls use hydroponics, domestic systems tend to be based on the idea of hanging bags of potting soil into which annuals or perennials are planted. The number of panels of bags can be increased as space allows, but the bags can be ugly to look at until the plants establish and obscure the plastic. Watering needs to be careful and regular.

Alternatively, with a little DIY, various systems can be constructed to hold plants, either on a wall or on a free-standing (well-secured) frame. The most straightforward of these is to use lengths of guttering. Once the gutters are fixed to the wall, and both ends capped off, fill them with potting soil. Gutter gardens are best used for fast-growing vegetable crops, such as salads and annual herbs, which can be sown and harvested and re-sown several times within the growing season.

A NOTE ON SHELF GARDENS

Single or multiple pots of plants can look very effective on a shelf, or even in box picture frames (make sure the wall fixings will take the weight). When grouping plants together, it's a good idea to use a designers' trick and have a unifying theme, such as keeping the pots all the same color (though size and shape may vary), or the foliage color the same, although it may take different forms.

WREATH GARDENS

Wreaths need not be confined to the front door at Christmas time: living wreaths can be made from succulents or moss, to create a miniature garden and an interesting focal point for a door or wall (they can be heavy, so fasten them well).

A CORK WREATH FOR THE FRIDGE

Old wine corks are brilliant planters for tiny succulents—champagne corks are even better! Here, by gluing small magnets to one side of the corks, they can be used to create a miniature garden on the fridge.

METHOD

Start by using the knife to hollow out the center of each cork to create a planting hole. Make the holes as big as possible without compromising the structural integrity of the sides and base of the cork. If possible, to avoid potential injury, use a vice to hold the cork.

Glue a magnet to each cork and leave to dry. Then use a spoon to add potting soil to each cork.

Plant a succulent in each cork, making sure they are firmly planted.

↓

Arrange the cork magnets in a wreath shape on the fridge, freezer, or any other magnetic surface.

MAINTENANCE

Water the plants regularly using a spray bottle or turkey baster.

TAKING CUTTINGS FROM SUCCULENTS

Many rosette-forming succulents produce miniature versions, known as offsets or pups, that can be carefully dug up (try to retain some roots) and replanted to create a new plant. Branching succulents can be propagated by cuttings: cut off a small section of stem and leave in a dry, sunny place until a callus has grown over the wound, then plant in fresh potting soil so it can form new roots and start to grow.

OFFSET

A STRING WREATH

Balls of string offer slightly larger planting holes than corks, and can therefore be used for larger plants, although it would still be advisable to use slow-growing succulents or cacti. This wreath could be made large or small, using neutral or brightly colored balls of twine.

METHOD

Plug the base of each ball of twine with some tightly wadded cotton wool then use the wire to fasten them to the wreath base securely, covering the whole base. The central holes of the twine balls need not be pointing directly upward, as long as the potting soil will not fall out.

Fill each ball of string with some potting soil and plant with a succulent or cactus.

YOU WILL NEED:

- Complete balls of garden twine, wrappers removed and ends tucked in
- Cotton wool
- Wire wreath base
- Thin wire
- Multipurpose potting soil
- Spoon
- Small succulent or cactus plants

MAINTENANCE

Water the plants regularly using a spray bottle. Place the wreath in bright light, but direct sunlight will cause it to dry out faster. The wreath would look attractive on any back door or shed door.

A SUCCULENT WREATH

For the maximum greenery in a wreath, dispense with the planters altogether. For a simpler, greener, alternative to succulents, just wire on more moss instead.

METHOD

Pack the wreath base with sphagnum moss as tightly as possible—this will be what the plants root into, so it needs to be secure and able to hold moisture. Wrap around with twine if necessary.

Take the succulents out of their pots and crumble away all the potting soil until there is only a small root ball left.

Pierce the base of the plant all the way through with a length of wire and affix it to the wreath base, laying the root ball on the moss (it will be covered by the foliage of the other plants). Continue with the plants until the whole base is covered and no root balls are visible. Any small rosettes or clumps of plants can also be attached, as they should sprout roots as well.

MAINTENANCE

Do not water for a month after planting to allow the plants to grow roots, then soak the whole thing. Attach a ribbon or wire to hang it on a door or wall.

CHAPTER 4

WATER AND WILDLIFE GARDENS

Even miniature gardens can create a bit of space for wildlife, giving real meaning to the saying "build it and they will come." Ponds can be as small as a bucket, or even a teacup. Create a garden in miniature—lawn, flower borders, and all—to attract bees and butterflies, and provide them with valuable nectar, or a miniature home for the miniature beasts of our world, the invertebrates.

MINIATURE PONDS

Although a miniature pond will be too small for fish or waterfowl to use, it will still provide valuable space for insects such as dragonflies, pond skaters, and water beetles to live and breed, and maybe even frogs, toads, and newts. It will also be a useful source of water for birds to drink from. Fill it with rainwater (see page 53) if possible, otherwise leave tap water to stand for a couple of days before planting.

SUITABLE CONTAINERS

Almost anything can be used to create a pond, from a bucket to a barrel or trough.

Make sure any holes are properly plugged, and that containers treated with any paints or preservatives have been thoroughly scrubbed and washed out on the inside. Fill wooden containers with water and keep topping up until the wood swells sufficiently to stop any small gaps (larger gaps may need to be filled in).

PLANTING A POND

Pond plants fall into three main categories; it's good to have at least one of each if there's space, as that will supply a good variety of wildlife habitats and keep the water healthy:

Marginal plants (e.g. rushes) are those that live in the soil at the edge of the pond where it is permanently damp. They protrude out of the water. The root ball should be just beneath the water's surface, so the plant may need to be placed on some form of shelf (a brick, for example) to raise it up.

Aquatic plants (e.g. water lilies) send their leaves up on long stems to float on the water's surface. They are anchored in a root ball in soil at the base of the pond. They help keep the water cool and provide shelter for water animals.

Oxygenators (e.g. water crowfoot) float in the water, submerged. They put oxygen into the water, and also provide shelter for the pond life.

SAFE ACCESS

If the pond is going to be large enough to accommodate amphibians and to attract birds and perhaps chipmunks looking for a drink, it's a good idea to provide easy access in and, more importantly, out of the pond with some form of ramp, to avoid drowning. The ramp should not be too steep and should have a rough surface for good grip: wrap wood in chicken wire or twine, for example.

METHOD

Planting is as simple as submerging the plants in aquatic baskets (perforated pots allowing the water to flow through the root ball, available at garden centers and specialist nurseries). These should be lined with burlap and planted up using heavy garden soil or proprietary aquatic potting soil (don't use normal multipurpose potting soil as it is too nutrient-rich and light for use in water).

Use stones or bricks under the basket to get marginal plants to the right height under the water and put water lilies on the bottom of the pond.

For very small ponds, the plants may have to be divided before planting.

MAINTENANCE

Clear away dead leaves/stems/flowers in late summer and fall. In spring, take each plant out of its basket and divide it into a manageable size.

PLANT FILE:
MINIATURE PONDS

Source pond plants from garden centers and specialist pond or fish nurseries.

MARGINAL PLANTS
(LESS THAN 2IN DEEP):
Sweet flag
(Acorus gramineus var. pusillus)
A tufted grass that grows 3–4in tall.

Brooklime
(Veronica beccabunga)
Has blue and white flowers and grows 4in tall.

MARGINAL PLANTS
(UP TO 6IN DEEP):
Bog arum
(Calla palustris)
Has white flowers then red berries (6–16in tall).

Water morning glory
(Ipomea aquatica)
Needs minimum temperatures of 50°F. Its leaves can be eaten like spinach. Grows up to 6in tall.

Water iris
(Iris laevigata)
Has blue flowers (28in tall).

Corkscrew rush
(Juncus effusus f. *spiralis)*
Has twisted stems (18in tall).

Water forget-me-not
(Myosotis scorpioides)
Has white flowers and needs water not more than 4in deep (12in tall).

Golden club
(Orontium aquaticum)
Has spikes of yellow flowers (4–10in tall).

Arrowhead, or duck potato
(Sagittaria latifolia)
Has edible tubers and needs soil 4in deep, then 6in water on top (20in+ tall).

FLOATING PLANTS
(4–12IN DEEP):
Frogbit
(Hydrocharis morsus-ranae)
Has small white flowers; the plant dies back in winter.

Water lily
(Nymphaea)
Nymphaea odorata var. *minor* has fragrant white flowers. *N.* 'Pygmaea Helvola' has yellow flowers and variegated leaves. *N.* 'Pygmaea Rubra' has pink flowers. *N. tetragona* 'Alba' has white flowers.

OXYGENATORS/
SUBMERGED PLANTS:
Water violet
(Hottonia palustris)
Has its leaves under water but purple flowers on the surface in spring.

Hair grass
(Eleocharis acicularis)
Forms an underwater lawn for ponds 2–12in deep.

HAIR GRASS

Bog arum (Calla palustris) has heart-shaped leaves and exotic-looking flowers in summer.

GARDENS FOR BEES AND BUTTERFLIES

Domestic gardens, no matter how big or small, are invaluable to wildlife to live and feed in, or as pit stops between home and other sources of food. By planting a scaled-down version, of lawns, borders, and all, even a miniature garden can provide some nectar and shelter to bees and butterflies.

Research by the University of Sheffield and the Royal Horticultural Society in the UK has discovered that bugs benefit most from having a wide range of different plant and flower types, and a long flowering season (both on individual plants and by a succession of different plants blooming over the year). Contrary to what was previously thought, it is not essential that these plants are native—in fact, by using plants from different regions, a wider range of plant types and flowering times can be achieved.

BUGS TO SPOT

HONEYBEE

Honeybees Hives can house up to 60,000 honeybees, which are ruled by a queen bee. Male bees (drones) stay in the hive to look after the larvae and build the honeycomb, while infertile female worker bees go out to collect the nectar.

Bumblebees There are around 25 different species of bumblebee, which have the Latin name *Bombus*. They live in nests of 100–200 bees, usually in the ground, trees, or potting soil heaps.

BUMBLEBEE

Solitary bees These bees live on their own, raising their young themselves over the summer. They will nest in the ground, or hollow plant stems or old wood; anywhere that provides dry shelter.

Hoverflies and lacewing flies These are valuable bugs in the garden, as their larvae feed on aphids. Lacewing larvae are black. Hoverflies have yellow and black stripes, but are easily distinguished from a bee or wasp by their characteristic hovering flight pattern.

HOVERFLIES

LACEWINGS

LADYBUG

Ladybugs How many spots? Ladybugs can have as few as two or as many as 24 spots. Their colors include cream, brown, red, and black. Most will live for a year, staying dormant over winter, and can eat around 5,000 aphids during their lifetime.

Butterflies and moths These prefer flowers with flat tops, such as daisies, but will gather nectar from a range of species. The markings on the different species, both on the butterfly/moth and the caterpillar, vary widely and are often brilliantly colorful. Look out for peacock, red admiral, and painted lady butterflies, and the polyphemus moth.

BUTTERFLIES
AND MOTHS

GARDEN IN A BOX

If you don't have a real back garden, create one in miniature within a single box, with all the plants chosen to attract bees and butterflies.

METHOD

Plant the garden in a box such as an old wooden wine box, to get a large surface area on top, and drill some drainage holes in the base. Avoid using metal boxes as they exaggerate the temperature, making the contents too hot in the sun and too cold in a frost.

YOU WILL NEED:
- Wooden box
- Multipurpose potting soil
- Clover plants, bulbs
- Empty snail shells

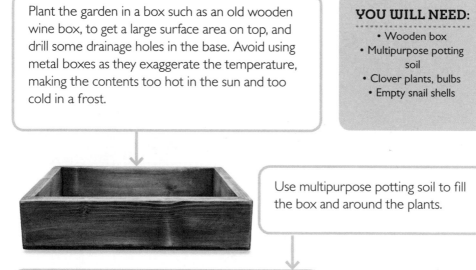

Use multipurpose potting soil to fill the box and around the plants.

Create a flowering lawn using clover plants—bees will love the flowers. Sow it from seed or dig up plants from a friend's lawn (many people see it as a weed and will be glad to get rid of it). Trim the plants once a month or so to keep them relatively low and to stop them invading the borders.

Plant up the borders in the box using small plants, for a good selection of flowers in spring, summer, and fall. Include bulbs for spring and fall, pushing them in to a depth of twice their height.

A tiny shallow pond, made from a submerged bowl or bottle cap, will provide the bugs with drinking water. Add stones to the bottom if necessary so it's not so deep that bugs could drown. Keep the water topped up and fresh.

Tiny succulent cuttings could be planted in a little potting soil in empty snail shells to create miniature "pots."

Put the box in as prominent a spot as possible so it will be visible to the bugs. It should also be in the sunshine, as many bugs rely on the sun's heat to keep warm and be able to fly. On a balcony, a double-sided window-box that fits over the railings could be used instead.

MAINTENANCE

Water the box well after planting and regularly to keep the potting soil moist. Apply a liquid feed fortnightly through the spring and summer. Never use pesticides on the plants when they are in flower, or the wildlife may also be harmed. Deadhead old flowers regularly to prolong the flowering season.

PLANT FILE:
WILDLIFE GARDENS

The Pollinator Partnership publishes ecoregional guides for planting. Visit their website (noted on page 140) and find the guide suitable for your region. These plants are all suited to a miniature wildlife garden, but most small plants will be beneficial. Just make sure that the flowers are not double (i.e. lots of petals obscuring the center) or the nectar will be inaccessible.

ANNUALS AND BIENNIALS

Busy Lizzie
(Impatiens)
The classic summer-flowering bedding plant will reach a height of 8in.

Lobelia
(Lobelia)
These trailing bedding plants flower in summer and with most of the plant over the side, won't take more than 8in of space.

Forget-me-not
(Myosotis species*)*
A biennial that will grow from seed one summer, then flower the following spring, reaching 6in tall.

French marigold
(Tagetes)
Tagetes 'Starfire', 'Golden Gate', and 'Mowgli Bicolor' are all smaller varieties (height 6in) of the summer-flowering plant.

Violets/pansies
(Viola)
These can flower from fall to spring in good conditions; height 6in.

BULBS

Crocus
(Crocus)
An early spring or fall flower of 4in tall (different varieties for each season).

Snowdrop
(Galanthus nivalis)
Invaluable early spring flowers, height 6in.

Hyacinth
(Hyacinthus orientalis)
Spring flowers reach 6in tall.

Grape hyacinth
(Muscari armeniacum)
Spring-flowering *Muscari armeniacum* (8in tall) or *Muscari azureum* (4in tall).

Daffodil
(Narcissus)
Spring flowers. Choose dwarf species/cultivars e.g. *N. bulbocodium* or *N.* 'Tête-à-tête' which are only 8–10in tall.

Autumn squil
(Scilla autumnalis)
A fall flower of 10in tall.

WILD VIOLET

Grape Hyacinth (*Muscari*) flowers provide valuable nectar to bees early in the season.

Butterflies like wide, flat heads (umbels) to land on, such as this sedum.

PLANT FILE:
WILDLIFE GARDENS (cntd.)

When choosing plants, aim for a good variety in order that there will be flowers in as many seasons as possible; the flowering season is given for each plant below. Remove old/dead flowers on annuals regularly to prolong the flowering of each plant.

PERENNIALS
Bugle
(Ajuga reptans)
Flowers from spring into summer at a height of 6in.

Thrift
(Armeria maritima)
A mounded plant of 6in, flowering in spring and summer.

Michaelmas daisy
(Aster 'Little Carlow')
A late summer/fall flowering plant that can be up to 20in tall. Cut back the stems by half in late May to keep it small.

Aubretia
(Aubretia)
A trailing, spring-flowering plant taking up 6in of space.

Heather
(Calluna and Erica)
Summer- and winter-flowering varieties available at heights of 8in.

Sedum
(Sedum)
Many rock-garden species are suitable, e.g. *Sedum spathulifolium* (2½in tall and summer flowers).

Lamb's ears
(Stachys byzantina)
Rosettes of furry leaves and flower spikes up to 20in tall in summer.

Edible plants
Pinks/carnations
(Dianthus)
Mounded foliage and edible flowers 20in tall in summer.

Alpine strawberry
(Fragaria vesca)
6in tall plants produce edible flowers and fruit all summer.

Oregano
(Origanum)
A 6in tall herb with edible foliage and edible flowers in summer.

Primroses and cowslips
(Primula)
Edible flowers in spring (height 4in).

Thyme
(Thymus vulgaris)
Edible flowers in summer and evergreen edible foliage 6in tall.

Consider planting some dwarf vegetables, too, as their flowers are popular with bees. Try dwarf French or broad beans, or sow baby carrots or parsnips and leave them in the pot until they flower the following summer.

THYME

GARDENS FOR MINIBEASTS

Bees and butterflies are easily the most visible insects in the garden, but the bugs that like to hide in the nooks and crannies, such as roly polys and beetles, are invaluable too.

Old pieces of branch or tree trunk are the perfect habitat for minibeasts, because they offer not only lots of crevices to hide in but also food in the form of the wood itself. Many of these bugs are essential to the decomposition of old plant material, helping to break it down and turn it back into the soil. Call a tree removal service to see if they have any older pieces of wood you can salvage, ideally one that is small enough to fit in the space available but also offers some larger nooks into which to put some plants.

Gardens that use old tree trunks as foils and areas for planting are known as stumperies. They do best in a cool, shady area. Suitable plants to use are ferns, moss, and other woodland plants—the smaller the plant to begin with, the more easily it will be planted into a gap in the wood.

YOU WILL NEED:

- A large piece of old wood
- Multipurpose potting soil
- Small plants and/or moss

METHOD

Put the wood in its final position before planting it.

Choose a hollow area in the wood that is big enough for a plant. Assess how much space there will be around the root ball and fill the base of the hole with potting soil accordingly, then put in the plant and fill around it, firming it in well with as much potting soil as will fit.

Repeat for as many hollows as possible, using plants, or firming in moss to smaller crevices.

Do not eat any fungi that might sprout from the wood as they are likely to be toxic to humans.

MAINTENANCE

Leave the wood undisturbed as much as possible.
Water using a turkey baster or small watering can.

The wood may already have had some minibeasts living in it, but more will be attracted to it.

MINIBEASTS TO HUNT FOR

Another name for minibeasts would be creepy-crawlies, but they are just small animals. The bugs that will come to live in the stumpery prefer the darker, damper areas of gardens and woodlands. The easiest way to spot them is to gently lift up the wood to look underneath, but don't do this too often or the bugs will move away from the continual disturbance.

Rotting wood can be home to a world of fungi, plants, and minibeasts.

Beetles Stag beetle larvae depend on rotting wood for food. The adult males are unmistakable with their large "antlers." The larvae of the eastern Hercules beetle also eat decaying wood, and take two years to become adults. The devil's coach horse beetle shelters in dark places, emerging at night to hunt.

Centipedes and millipedes The carnivorous centipede is much faster than the millipede, which lives off decaying vegetation. Both will benefit from a minibeast garden, for food and shelter.

Slugs and snails These hide in damp, dark places during the heat of the day and emerge at dusk to feed. If they are eating the plants on the stumpery, it may be best to relocate them. They have a homing instinct, but take them far enough away and it will be a while before they return!

Spiders Easily spotted around their webs, garden spiders may also take shelter in the minibeast mansion.

Roly polys These little gray animals prefer damp, shady places where they will not get too hot and dry. They feed on rotting plant matter, and are invaluable in the ecosystem to help recycle the nutrients back into the soil.

CHAPTER 5

PRODUCTIVE GARDENS

Even the smallest of gardens can provide something to eat or drink, but when space is limited it's best to grow crops with the maximum effect on the plate. Micro-leaves pack a big flavor punch relative to their size, and their different colors can be sown to create a picture—growing by numbers, as it were. Other crops, such as herbs and strawberries, taste significantly better harvested fresh and ripe, so it's worth growing them even in miniature. Finally, rather than throwing away the leafy top of a pineapple, why not grow it as an unusual houseplant? Given the right conditions, it may even produce another fruit!

HERB GARDENS

Cinder blocks—the large cement bricks with two large holes in them—make great urban or industrial-look planters, and can be stacked up to create more space for planting.

This herb garden would fit easily against a sunny wall or along one side of a balcony for a ready supply of fresh herbs to use in the kitchen.

YOU WILL NEED:
....
- One or more cinder blocks (hollow dense concrete blocks) of approximately 17 $\frac{5}{16}$in x 8 $\frac{7}{16}$in x 8 $\frac{7}{16}$in
- Multipurpose potting soil
- One or more herb plants in 3½in pots
- Trowel
- Watering can

METHOD

Stack up the blocks, taking care to align them properly so they are stable, and not going more than four blocks high. Pyramids offer a good number of planting holes, but any number of variations is possible.

Fill each available hole with multipurpose potting soil, leaving a 1in lip at the top. If a number of blocks on top of each other has created a deep well, the bottom can be filled in with large stones or even broken up polystyrene to save on potting soil and reduce the weight.

Plant one herb in each hole and water in well.

MAINTENANCE

The planting holes are not large, so the herbs will need regular watering to avoid the potting soil drying out completely. Add the water a little at a time, allowing it to sink in before pouring on more, so that it does not wash away.

If the plants are regularly cut to use in the kitchen they will not need much pruning. Trim back to just above where the stems turn from brown at the base to green once they have flowered in summer to keep them compact and fresh. It is best to replace them every three years or so.

PLANT FILE:
HERB GARDEN

For a cinder-block garden, choose plants that prefer free-draining soil, as they will best tolerate the small growing area. Mediterranean herbs originate from countries with dry, sunny climates and tend to prefer growing in loose scree rather than moist soil, so these are ideal. Consider how the plants will look together once planted and select upright, bushy, or trailing plants appropriately.

Rosemary
(*Rosemarinus officinalis*)

Evergreen, with small, narrow dark green leaves, and extremely versatile in the kitchen. The basic form is *Rosmarinus officinalis*, but the variety 'Miss Jessop's Upright' is an even more upright shape. Alternatively, *Rosmarinus officinalis Prostratus Group* is a trailing variety.

Thyme
(*Thymus*)

Evergreen, low-growing bushes, most thymes form neat little mounds of foliage. *Thymus vulgaris* is the common thyme, but the lemon-scented type is also worth having. Some forms have larger, glossier leaves than the small, narrow dark green leaves of common thyme, or even golden-variegated foliage. *Thymus serpyllum* is a creeping, mat-forming thyme.

Lavender
(*Lavandula*)

While less commonly used in the kitchen, lavender is ideal for this situation. *Lavandula angustifolia* has the classic scent/flavor—try a compact variety such as 'Hidcote', or a white-flowered type. Butterfly lavender (*Lavandula stoechas*) flowers earlier in the summer but is not quite as hardy, and can't be used in cooking—it is poisonous.

Oregano/marjoram
(*Origanum*)

This closely related family includes sweet marjoram (*Origanum marjorana*) and Italian oregano (*Origanum* x *majoricum*), but the best option for miniature gardens is the compact form of oregano, *Origanum vulgare* 'Compactum'.

Chamomile
(*Chamaemelum*)

This low-growing, bright green plant is ideal for miniature gardens. For flowers, choose the basic form *Chamaemelum nobile*, but for a chamomile lawn or seat (see page 36), get the non-flowering variety 'Treneague'.

Scented geraniums
(*Pelargonium*)

These come in a variety of fragrances, from lemon to rose to cinnamon. They will require a little more water than the other herbs, but are good to use in baking, and easy to grow from cuttings (see page 15).

LAVENDER

Rosemary
(*Rosmariunus officinalis*)
can be used in
myriad savoury and
sweet dishes.

STRAWBERRY TOWER

Strawberries are one of the easiest and most rewarding fruits to grow. The plants take up little room, need little attention, and the fruit tastes so much better plucked warm and ripe from the plant.

ALPINE VARIETY

Strawberries produce new baby plants every year, so there's no need to buy another plant ever again! Stack pots on top of each other to build a high-rise strawberry tower, and pick the berries as they cascade down the sides.

WHAT TO PLANT

Strawberries produce fruit either all in one flush, or (fewer) berries spread over many months, known as perpetual or everbear types. However, it's possible to spread the harvests of the single-flush types over the summer by choosing three or more different varieties that fruit in early, mid, and late season. Alternatively, include alpine strawberries; the tiny fruits that are great to add to drinks (these would be best planted in the top pot). All strawberries should be left on the plant until they are fully red. Pick them when they are warmed by sunshine for the best flavor.

- Early season varieties: 'Honeoye'
- Mid-season varieties: 'Cambridge Favorite', 'Alice', 'Pegasus'
- Late-season varieties: 'Symphony', 'Florence'
- Perpetual varieties: 'Mara des Bois', 'Aromel'

METHOD

Fill the large pot three-quarters full of potting soil and tap the base on the ground to settle the potting soil, then put the medium pot on top. Fill in the large pot with more potting soil, leaving a lip of 1–1¼in from the top. Fill the medium pot three-quarters full and place the small pot on top.

YOU WILL NEED:

- At least 3 (terracotta) pots—one small, one medium, and one large
- Bamboo cane or similar stake
- Multipurpose potting soil
- 9 strawberry plants
- Trowel
- Watering can

Push the bamboo cane down through the drainage hole in the bottom of the small pot, straight down through the medium pot until it hits the bottom of the large pot. Cut off the top so the cane will be buried in the potting soil of the small pot. Fill in around the medium pot and fill the small pot to the top (again leaving a lip).

Plant the strawberry plants into the potting soil: put one in the top pot, three evenly spaced around the edge of the middle pot, and five evenly spaced around the edge of the bottom pot. Water them in well.

MAINTENANCE

The plants will need regular watering—make sure each pot is watered thoroughly. Aim to keep the potting soil consistently moist, especially as the berries start to grow, as irregular watering will lead to misshapen fruit.

Apply an all-purpose or tomato liquid feed once they start to flower and until they finish fruiting, following the instructions on the label.

Perhaps most important, to avoid losing the precious strawberries to the birds or other pests, is to protect them as the berries start to ripen and redden. Simply cover the whole tower loosely with a piece of netting (making sure the strawberries don't protrude), tucking the ends under the pot or weighing them down with other pots or large stones.

Remove dead leaves, bare fruit stems, and any rotten fruit as they appear.

MAKING NEW STRAWBERRY PLANTS

Plants reproduce themselves in two ways. Some produce seeds, and can only create new versions of themselves this way. Others produce seeds but also propagate themselves vegetatively—that is, a part of the plant makes new roots for itself and grows into a new plant.

In mid to late summer, strawberry plants start to produce "runners," long stems with small plants along them that trail away from the main plant looking for new soil into which to root. Take two or three of these runners and pin (half a paperclip works well) the first little plant on each runner into its own little pot of moist potting soil.

Cut the runner off beyond the little plant, but leave it attached to the main plant. Leave them to produce roots and more leaves, keeping the potting soil moist, then cut them off from the main plant as well. The new strawberry plants can be transferred to a larger pot or the ground in the spring.

TEAPOT

Teapots make great little planters, and are ideal for growing a miniature herbal tea plantation. They will need careful watering, though, as obviously they have no drainage.

YOU WILL NEED:
- A teapot
- Herb plant (in a small pot, or a cutting)
- Multipurpose potting soil
- Spoon
- Small watering can or bottle

METHOD

Make sure the teapot is completely clean by washing it out with washing-up liquid, as any lurking bacteria could infect and rot the plant.

Unless the teapot is very large, it will be a bit of a squeeze to get even a herb in a 3½in pot into the opening, so either split the plant down, or take a cutting. Either way, plant the herb into the teapot and fill around it almost up to the top with the potting soil—it will be easier to do this with a spoon than a trowel.

WATERING THE TEAPOT

As with most plants, the herbs will like being in consistently moist, but not wet, potting soil. However, as the teapot has no drainage, be very careful not to overwater it; in a hot spot the potting soil may appear dry on the surface but be sodden at the bottom. Check the moisture level as deep as possible into the potting soil before adding any water by sticking a finger or wooden skewer into it.

MAKING HERBAL TEAS

Pick a couple of small sprigs and check for any dirt or wildlife (rinse under the tap if necessary), then put into a mug or teacup. Once the kettle has boiled, leave it to stand for a minute or two before pouring over the herbs, otherwise they will be burned by the scalding water. Leave to infuse and cool to drinking temperature (add a splash of cold water to speed this up).

MINT

LEMON VERBENA

CHAMOMILE

TO SPLIT A POTTED PLANT

Most herbaceous plants—anything with multiple stems and a fibrous root ball—can be split into multiple plants. The smaller the plant to begin with, the fewer times it can be divided and the longer it will take to grow into a substantial plant. For a miniature garden, divide a plant in a 3½in pot into two or three sections.

1 Take the plant out of its pot, ensuring that it has been well watered a few hours previously.

2 Assess where the stems are, and how many times it would be most easily divided, then gently prise the root ball apart and tease out the roots by hand.

3 It's inevitable that some of the root ball will be lost, but so long as each stem has roots attached, it should re-establish well once planted into the teapot.

Lemon balm (*Melissa officinalis*) has a lovely lemon scent and makes a delicious tea.

PLANT FILE:
TEA

Many herbs will make good herbal teas, but the most easily grown, and most delicious, are listed here. The heights given are the potential size of a mature plant: growing from cuttings and regular picking of the leaves for tea will help keep the plants miniature for longer, and the foliage young and fresh.

Mint
(Mentha)
The best varieties for making tea are peppermint (*Mentha x piperita*) and spearmint (*Mentha spicata*). Moroccan mint (*Mentha spicata* var. *crispa* 'Moroccan') is good for the sweetened mint teas of that country. (Ultimate height 3¼ft.)

Lemon balm
(Melissa officinalis)
On its own (it has a lemon sherbet flavor) or mixed with mint, lemon balm (*Melissa officinalis*) makes a great tea that is said to help lift the spirits. (Ultimate height 3¼ft.)

Chamomile
(Chamaemelum nobile)
Excellent to aid sleep, chamomile (*Chamaemelum nobile*) is a low-growing plant that will cascade over the edges of the teapot. Pick the flowers only for making tea. (Ultimate height 10in.)

Lemon verbena
(Aloysia citrodora)
Lemon verbena (*Aloysia citrodora*) can form a very large shrub, but a cutting grown in a teapot and frequently cut back for tea leaves can be kept small for some time. (Ultimate height 2–3ft.)

Lemongrass
(Cymbopogon citratus)
Lemongrass (*Cymbopogon citratus*) looks like… well, a grass, and will shoot up and then arch gracefully downward. The thick shoots/roots clumped at the base can be separated from the main plant to cook with, but the leaves make a good tea as well. (Ultimate height 5ft.)

LEMON VERBENA

MICRO-LEAVES PICTURE

Many people will remember growing cress "hair" for an eggshell "head" as children, but with the variety of colors and leaf shapes now available to grow as micro-leaves, far more intricate and ambitious pictures are possible. Of course, eggshells could also be used— perhaps a line of them in egg cups, each with a different hair color?

A SEED HAS ALL IT NEEDS

Seeds sprinkled on damp kitchen paper or cotton wool are able to start growing just as well as those sown into potting soil or soil. This is because the seeds have all the nutrients and energy they need within themselves in order to start growing; all they need to activate growth is water. Once the seed germinates and exhausts this food store, its tiny root and shoot can start collecting nutrients and photosynthesizing to make the food it needs to continue growing.

RED CABBAGE SPROUTS

METHOD

Fill the tray evenly with seed-starting mix and press it down gently, then water it thoroughly. Alternatively, line it with three or four sheets of kitchen paper and soak them well. For eggshells, fill almost to the top with potting soil (and water them) or damp cotton wool instead of potting soil.

With the image for the picture in mind   or sketched on a piece of paper or stencil—scatter the seeds over the potting soil/paper. They should be quite close together but not touching, in a single layer.

YOU WILL NEED:

- A shallow plastic tray (e.g. those containing vegetables or fruit at the supermarket) or empty, clean eggshells with the tops removed
- Multipurpose potting soil, cotton wool, or a few sheets of kitchen paper/towel
- Trowel or spoon
- Salad/vegetable seeds
- Small watering can
- Spray bottle

MAINTENANCE

Put the tray on a sunny windowsill and keep the surface of the seed-starting mix or the kitchen paper moist at all times by spraying it with a misting bottle (this will probably need doing at least once a day).

Harvest the seedlings before they develop another set of leaves—these will be visible emerging at the top of the stem, between the first set of leaves—by cutting the stems with a pair of scissors. Use them to garnish any savory dish.

Micro salad
leaves are
available in mixes,
as well as
individual types.

PLANT FILE:
SALAD LEAF VARIETIES

There are seed mixes available to grow specifically as micro-leaves, but all salad leaf, lettuce, and herb seeds are suitable, as well as many vegetable seeds. If you are making a micro-leaves picture it's better to have single varieties of seed that can be used in specific areas. It's a good way to use up leftover seed at the end of the growing season. Below are some suggestions for the various colors that could be used:

BRIGHT GREEN FOLIAGE
Mustard
(Brassica juncea)
Good varieties include 'Green Frills'.

Carrot
(Daucus carota)
Any carrot variety will be fine.

Mizuna/mibuna
(Brassica rapa/B. rapa var. nipposinica)
No named varieties.

Fennel
(Foeniculum vulgare/Foeniculum vulgare var. azoricum)
Either herb or bulb fennel would work well.

MID-GREEN FOLIAGE
Rocket
(Eruca vesicaria)
Either wild rocket or other varieties will work.

Radish
(Raphanus sativa)
Any variety is suitable.

Coriander
(Coriandrum sativum)
The basic form or a variety is suitable.

Swede
(Brassica napus Napobrassica Group)
Use any variety.

Sunflower
(Helianthus annuus)
Any variety is suitable.

Spinach/chard
(Spinacia oleracea/Beta vulgaris subsp. cicla var. flavescens)
Any type of these leafy vegetables will work well.

DARK GREEN FOLIAGE
Kale
(Brassica oleracea Acephala Group)
The variety 'Red Russian' is a good choice.

Mustard
(Brassica juncea)
Good varieties include 'Red Frills'.

PURPLE FOLIAGE
Amaranth
(Amaranthus)
'Red Army' is a good variety.

Basil
(Ocimum basilicum)
Use 'Purple Ruffles' or 'Dark Opal' for good purple leaves.

PINEAPPLE GROVE

Pineapples have an interesting way of reproducing themselves: their leafy top grows into a new plant. Take advantage of this to create a miniature grove from what would otherwise be kitchen scraps. A long, rectangular planter of pineapple crowns would make a great table centerpiece.

YOU WILL NEED:

- A glass of water
- Wooden skewers or toothpicks
- Pot/planter
- Multipurpose potting soil
- Grit
- One or more pineapples
- Trowel
- Watering can

When buying the pineapple, choose one (or more) with a healthy-looking crop of leaves—they should be green, firm and have no signs of pest infestation or mold. The pineapple itself should be ripe, but not overripe.

METHOD

Hold the pineapple firmly, and grasp the leaves at the base. Twist them up and out of the fruit. Strip off some of the lower leaves, to leave a stub of stem about 2in long, then leave the whole thing somewhere dry and bright. This allows the wounds on the stem to heal over, and reduces the risk of the crown rotting when planted. It may be possible to see tiny bumps on the stem—this is from where the new roots will grow.

Fill a glass of water, then suspend the crown in it so that the leafless part is under water but the leaves remain dry. If the glass is narrow enough, the leaves can keep it suspended; otherwise, use wooden skewers or toothpicks inserted into the stem to balance the crown over the top of the glass.

Put the glass on a sunny, warm windowsill. Change the water every couple of days and wait for roots to form (this can take several weeks).

Once there is a healthy crop of roots at least 2–4in long on the stem, prepare the pot/planter with a mix of multipurpose potting soil and grit, in a ratio of 4:1, and carefully plant the crown, submerging all the roots but not the leaves. Water it well.

MAINTENANCE

Keep the pineapple(s) in a sunny, warm place (not below 64°F). It will also need relatively humid air around it—a bathroom or busy kitchen is ideal, or mist it regularly if it's in a centrally heated room.

Water to keep the soil just moist, and apply fertilizer once a month in spring and summer.

In good conditions, the crowns can produce more pineapples, but it may take several years, so it's perhaps best to just enjoy the glaucous, spiky foliage.

CHAPTER 6

MINIATURE GARDENING BASICS

From planting to watering, and dealing with any problems that might arise, this chapter details the basics of gardening in miniature. Gardening is not a technical or a mystical pastime, and there is no such thing as green fingers. Plants do not have the capacity to not grow out of spite. All they want from you are the basics: somewhere to grow, some sunshine, and some water. Understand and provide this, and your garden, however miniature, will thrive.

PLANTING MINIATURE GARDENS

Gardening in miniature is in many ways simpler than full-scale gardening, and requires no expertise. Just a few simple tools and supplies are all that are needed for planting.

EQUIPMENT

Miniature gardens do not require a lot of equipment, and many tools can be substituted with simple household utensils to minimize the outlay. These are the most useful:

Pots and containers will vary according to the type of garden. Some will require drainage holes, others will be better without them. For planting outside, ensure the container is frost-proof (new pots should indicate on the label whether they are safe in low temperatures). They should also be clean: wash out with hot, soapy water, rinse, and dry before use.

Saucers and trays are handy for standing pots with drainage holes on so they don't leave water stains on the surfaces on which they are placed.

A trowel is useful for transferring potting soil from the bag to the container and for planting, although a spoon is easier for very small pots.

Pruners are the best tool for cutting small branches, such as when taking hardwood cuttings or gathering lichened branches (see pages 56–57). Keep them sharp, clean, and rust-free. Sharp kitchen scissors will suffice for all other cutting.

Watering cans are available in many sizes and styles; the best choice will vary with the type of miniature garden. Often a plastic bottle with a small screw-on breaker (a perforated flat head to fit over the spout/top, available in garden centers and online) will be more than adequate. The easier it is to control the water flow, the better the watering can.

A spray bottle is an alternative for watering plants that require humid air or not much water; these are widely available in garden centers. Make sure the nozzle can be turned to supply a single jet or fine mist of water.

POTTING SOIL AND OTHER SUPPLIES

Many of the gardens do not need specialist planting substrates: multipurpose potting soil is absolutely fine, but it may be necessary to pick out a few larger pieces of bark, or to sieve it before use to create a finer mix. Buy the best available brand that is affordable, preferably peat-free and organic.

For a finer-grade potting soil, choose those labeled as suitable for seed-sowing. Other specialist potting soils, required by one or two gardens, are cactus potting soil (easily created by mixing two parts potting soil with one part fine gravel or grit); carnivorous plant potting soil (available online); and bonsai potting soil/akadama (also available online).

Small gravel or grit is also useful for mixing with potting soil to create a faster-draining planting medium, for drainage layers and attractive mulches. If this is gathered from outside, first wash and sterilize it by dousing in boiling water.

BUYING PLANTS

Only ever buy healthy-looking plants, free from obvious pest and disease infestations and with strong (green) growth. Turn the plant out of its pot to check the roots as well—they should fill the pot but not be wound round and round the inside (root-bound).

When purchasing plants online, ensure the site has a no-quibbles return policy. Open the parcel as soon as possible and put the plants in the light and give them plenty of water to recover from the stress of the journey.

For miniature gardens, it's best to buy plants in 3½in pots or smaller (3½in refers to the diameter of the top of the pot, and is a standard size of small potted plants). Some garden centers and nurseries will stock plants in miniature pots; alternatively, search online for retailers.

HOW TO PLANT

When putting a plant into a container of potting soil (or other planting medium), ensure the hole is big enough to take the root ball. The top of the root ball should be flush with the potting soil surface once it is firmed in.

Always firm a plant into its planting medium well, ensuring the root ball is in good contact with the potting soil around it so that the roots can begin to expand outward and take up moisture from the surrounding potting soil. However, press downward around the root ball, rather than directly around the base of the stem(s), to avoid breaking the roots away from the stems.

MAINTAINING MINIATURE GARDENS

Understanding how plants grow and a few basic principles of plant science is the key to being a good miniature gardener. Plants are not complicated, and neither is keeping them in good health.

WHAT A PLANT NEEDS TO GROW WELL

Plants are able to manufacture their own food, making their own source of energy, in a process called photosynthesis. This takes place in all the green parts of a plant—where there are cells containing a green substance called chlorophyll.

In order for photosynthesis to occur, the gardener needs only to supply the plant with three things: water, sunlight, and carbon dioxide. The plant will do the rest.

Light is therefore crucial for a plant to grow well, so always put the miniature garden in the best spot as specified for each garden. Some will prefer direct sunlight, others bright but indirect light, others even prefer a little shade, but all need some light.

LIGHT + WATER + CARBON DIOXIDE = GLUCOSE + OXYGEN

PHOTOTROPISM

Most indoor plants only have light from one direction, unless the room is multi-aspect, and all will grow toward this light source. This may be a gradual process, or obvious in a matter of hours (such as with the salad seedlings, see page 115). Hormones in the plant stems cause the cells on the dark side to elongate, and the cells on the light side to shrink, enabling it to bend and capture the most light in its leaves. This is called phototropism.

Indoor containers, and pots placed outdoors next to a wall or fence, will therefore need regular rotating to ensure that the sun reaches all parts of the plants and the growth is even. How often this is required depends on how fast the plants are growing.

LEAF SCORCH

Plants placed too close to a heat source, or in direct sunlight (especially when intensified by a layer of glass, such as in a terrarium), may suffer from scorched leaves, when the edges of the leaves turn brown and crispy. This can also occur if the plants are exposed to extreme cold, such as a frost.

PRUNING

Although many of the plants specified are slow-growing and require little or no pruning, some work may be required here and there. Pruning is simply the removal of unwanted plant material. It falls into three main groups:

Removing the 4 "D"s: Dead, Dying, Diseased, and Duplicate stems or branches. These (especially the first three) should be removed from all plants, regardless of its overall pruning requirements, when they are first seen. Duplicate branches are those that cross or overlay each other and can be taken back to a suitable point if desired.

Cutting back herbaceous (non-woody) plants that have died back for winter. Some perennials retreat all their energy into the roots for winter, and all above-ground growth will die off. This can be cut off, to as low a point as possible on the stem, in fall or winter.

Trimming to restrict and reduce growth, and to keep plants looking neat and tidy, can be carried out on some plants. In general, plants will grow in order to keep the ratio of their roots and shoots in balance. By restricting the roots, the top-growth will also be restricted. However, some pruning may still be necessary, and this should be carried out as specified for each garden.

Whichever type of pruning is being carried out, always use clean, sharp tools, remove everything that is cut off, and cut just above a bud.

WEEDING

It is inevitable that even the most miniature of gardens may get some weeds. Most weeds are also classified as wildflowers—it is only a weed if it is growing where it is not wanted. Assuming it isn't wanted, remove it as soon as possible, ensuring all the roots as well as the shoots are taken out.

Typical sources of weeds are non-sterile soil or potting soil (i.e. that used from a garden rather than bought in a bag), which may contain weed seeds and/or pieces of weed root that regenerate; seeds or bits of grass root in sphagnum moss gathered from a lawn; and the wind or birds dropping seeds into pots outside.

MEADOW "WEEDS"

WATERING

Watering is perhaps the single most important task of a gardener, yet despite its simplicity, it is the one most often got wrong, weakening the plant and therefore making it susceptible to further infection by pests or diseases.

However water is given to a plant, add it a little at a time, allowing it to soak in before seeing if more is needed to make it moist all the way through. Get the spout or breaker as close as possible to the base of the plant, watering the roots, not the leaves. The exception is, of course, spraying (misting) the foliage of plants such as *Tillandsia* or moss.

Where specific plant groups prefer different conditions, such as the boggy soil required by carnivorous plants, this is detailed in the individual gardens, but the guide on the page opposite applies to most plants.

Containers with no drainage require a little more care, as it is easy to overwater them. Check, if possible, the moisture level in the potting soil as low down as possible—there may be a sodden layer below a dry crust that needs to dry out before more water is applied.

WHEN TO WATER

There is no great secret to watering plants, but it is crucial to check regularly whether they need water. This checking will prevent both under- and overwatering. Check the plant by putting a finger into the potting soil (if possible) to determine its moisture level. If this is not possible, take into account the appearance of the plant and potting soil, its position and environment, and when it was last watered.

A plant that needs water will have dry potting soil. Its leaves, and possibly stems, may have started to wilt and yellow (generally the lowest, oldest leaves will turn yellow first). Any flowers may dry up and drop off and new leaves will be smaller. Water it now!

A happy plant has moist, but not wet, potting soil. Its leaves and stems are green and turgid, and it looks healthy. Check again tomorrow.

An overwatered plant may also be drooping and yellowing, but this is because its roots are drowning in soggy, sodden potting soil. There may even be water visible in the drainage layer of a terrarium or pot saucer. Remove any water from a saucer and allow the pot to dry out to optimum level. It may even be possible to tip excess water out of a terrarium by tilting it carefully and holding down the planting layers.

CACTI PREFER FREE-DRAINED SOIL, SO ENSURE THEY ARE NOT OVERWATERED.

FEEDING

Giving a plant fertilizer—additional nutrients to help it grow—is essential for most pot-grown plants. It is also known as feeding a plant. Potting soil has only enough nutrition in it to feed the plant for a maximum of six months, and if no fertilizer is then added to the pot, the plant will suffer from nutrient deficiencies, weakening and potentially killing it.

WHEN TO FEED PLANTS

Plants only need fertilizer during their growing season—from spring to late summer. How often to apply it in this period depends on the type of fertilizer and the type of plant. See the specific miniature garden details and the application information on the packet for more guidance.

THE NUTRIENTS PLANTS NEED

Plants need a full range of nutrients, some in large quantities and some in trace amounts. The most important are nitrogen (N) for green leafy growth, phosphorus (P) for root development, and potassium (K) for helping flowering and fruiting. These three are always detailed on the label of fertilizers in a ratio of N:P:K—those formulated to aid flowering and fruiting, for example rose or tomato feed, will have more K than N or P, while lawn feeds will have a higher N value. General-purpose feeds have a more even ratio and should also supply all the other nutrients.

TYPES OF FERTILIZER

Fertilizers are available in liquid or granular forms. Liquid feeds are fast-acting but short-term and need applying more frequently. They are also the easiest to apply, as they are mixed with water. Granular forms are controlled- (often called slow-) release and so feed plants over a longer period once mixed in with the potting soil, but the results are also slower to materialize and they are not suitable for addressing a deficiency. Organic fertilizers are widely available.

DOSAGE

Always follow the guidelines on the packet. Although it is tempting to give plants a boost with extra fertilizer, too much can become toxic for the plants.

HOW TO FEED PLANTS

Never feed a plant that is desperate for water. Make sure the soil is moist through before applying fertilizer. Mix liquid fertilizers in with a usual can of water; scatter granules in with the potting soil when planting, or over the surface of the potting soil, raking in gently.

PESTS

Pests are animals that damage plants. They could be tiny bugs or large dogs. Protecting the plants from pests is not always possible. Generally, gardens outside will be at greater risk than those inside.

PREVENTION IS BETTER THAN CURE

Keeping plants healthy—well-watered, fertilized, and in the right position—will help them fight off attacks from bugs and other pests. Catching an infestation early increases the chances of getting rid of it entirely, so check plants regularly. It's also crucial to check any other plants that are in the house, or being brought into the house, for pests that could spread to the miniature gardens. Use chemical pesticides only as a last resort, after trying physical control methods, and always select a treatment that's recommended for the problem. Read the label and make sure that all manufacturer's instructions are followed, including maximum dose, spray, and harvest intervals.

MAMMALS

Dogs and cats can eat plants or knock over pots. Squirrels can dig up potting soil in pots or knock them over. Aside from placing pots out of reach and making sure they are secure, there is little in the way of prevention or cure available.

BIRDS

Birds will try to eat berries and other crops, and may flick potting soil out of pots. Fruit and vegetables can be protected with netting, making sure that there are no gaps through which a small bird could fit (and/or get trapped).

SLUGS AND SNAILS

Easy to spot from the damage they do (eaten leaves and flowers) and the shiny slime trails they leave, slugs and snails can lay waste to several plants in a single night. Physically removing the slugs and snails is the best policy. Check the plants at dusk and dawn, and in their hiding places, too—under pots and other shady, cool spots. Slug pellets are the most effective control but use them sparingly, as recommended on the instructions—overdosing is unnecessary, wasteful, and can be a hazard to pets and wildlife.

Ladybugs and
their larvae eat aphids,
so attract them to
the garden with flowers
(see page 18).

BUGS

Aphids (greenfly, blackfly) and whitefly consume the sap from plants, weakening them, and excrete a sticky, shiny solution onto the leaves. They tend to cluster around fresh, new growth at the tips of shoots and on the undersides of leaves. Small infestations are easily dealt with by hand, as they can be washed, rubbed, wiped, or sprayed off with water (blast robust plants with the shower) or a dilute solution of washing-up liquid. Make sure they go down the drain, though, as any left on the potting soil surface will simply climb back up. Cut off and destroy badly affected growth or treat larger infestations with an appropriate pesticide. Always follow the instructions for safe use. It may help to move cleaned houseplants outside for a bit, but only when it is warm enough to do so.

Mealybug and scale insects are harder to shift and may need picking, rubbing, or washing off one by one. Their waxy coats make them impervious to any water-based control.

Caterpillars are easy to spot, and once removed will not cause any further problems, although it may be better to cut damaged stems back to healthy growth to avoid infection of the weakened tissue.

For more information on identifying plant pests, see Further Resources (page 140).

DISEASES

Most plant diseases are fungal—types of rot—and this is especially true of plants grown in pots, which tend to be grown closer together and/or indoors, where air circulation is restricted and the more humid conditions foster fungal growth.

A HEALTHY ENVIRONMENT

As with preventing pests, infection is much less likely on healthy plants, so look after the miniature gardens well. Good housekeeping is also important to avoid cultivating an atmosphere in which disease could take hold, and to avoid spreading any existing disease. Molds and mildews are usually prevented by making sure there is adequate air flow.

Keep plants tidy, removing dead leaves and other detritus around the base of the plant. Make sure tools and equipment—including the pots themselves—are clean by washing with soap or other detergent and hot water. If the potting soil develops mold on its surface, repot the plant, washing off the roots entirely before replanting in fresh potting soil.

Fungicidal sprays are available to treat some diseases, but are best reserved for only when they are absolutely necessary. Select a treatment that is recommended for the disease that has been identified and always read the label before choosing a product. Make sure all manufacturer's instructions are followed, including maximum dose, spray, and harvest intervals.

Botrytis (gray mold) Spores of this fungus are present everywhere in the air, and will easily infect damaged or dead plant tissue, and then spread to live growth. Check the foliage at the base of plants regularly, especially in humid or damp conditions, and remove infected parts of the plant promptly and as carefully as possible.

Mildews The two main types of mildew, powdery and downy, are both easily preventable. Avoid infection by keeping plants healthy, with good air circulation around them and, crucially, not water-stressed by watering correctly. Humid and damp environments will foster the diseases, characterized by patches of white mold on the leaves that can quickly spread to the rest of the plant. Remove affected parts as soon as it's seen.

Viruses These are more commonly introduced in the plant itself, rather than through the environment. There is no cure for an infected plant, though you may be able to get a refund. Destroy the plant to prevent infection spreading to other plants of the same type.

For more information on identifying plant diseases, see Further Resources (page 140).

GLOSSARY

Annual A plant that completes its life cycle within a year, growing from seed to flowering and then dying off.

Biennial A plant that puts on foliage in the first year of growth, overwinters, and then flowers and dies in the second year.

Cutting A small piece of stem and leaves removed from the plant and potted in order that it will produce roots and grow into a new plant. Plants multiplied in this way will be genetically identical.

Dormant When a plant stops growing, e.g. over winter, but does not die. Or, when referring to seeds, a means of the seed surviving over a (long) time, so that it will not germinate until the conditions are favorable.

Ecosystem All living things that interact with each other and their physical environment within a given area.

Germination When a seed takes in water and grows a root and shoot.

Gravitropism (also called geotropism) The response of a plant to the stimulus of gravity. Roots display positive gravitropism, growing downward into the soil; shoots display negative gravitropism, growing upward toward the light.

Hardy A plant is called "hardy" when it will happily survive temperatures below 32°F.

Herbaceous A perennial plant whose top growth dies back in fall and shoots anew in spring is called herbaceous.

Hydroponics A system of growing plants in a stream of water and soluble nutrients rather than soil or potting soil, typically utilized for green walls.

Kokedama The Japanese art of displaying plants in mud and moss balls rather than pots.

Perennial A plant that continues to grow year on year (as opposed to an annual).

Photosynthesis The process by which plants create their own food using sunlight, water, and carbon dioxide.

Phototropism The response of a plant to the stimulus of light, whereby hormones cause the plant stems to bend to expose the leaves to the most sunlight.

Root ball The roots of the plant and the potting soil or soil that surrounds them once they are removed from the pot or ground.

Runner A long shoot interspersed with tiny plantlets put out by plants such as strawberries as a means of propagating themselves.

Terrarium A glass vessel containing plants that can be sealed so the plants form an ecosystem within the container.

Three and a half inch pot A standard-sized pot in which small plants are supplied; the measurement refers to the diameter of the pot.

FURTHER RESOURCES

The Pollinator Partnership website has a tremendous amount of information about gardening for the benefit of wildlife and pollinators: www.pollinator.org

The National Wildlife Foundation provides information about how to start a habitat garden: www.nwf.org

Many specialist nurseries have plant care information on their websites, such as aquatic and carnivorous plant nurseries. Some plant groups also have societies

dedicated to promoting the attractions of those plants, such as cacti and succulents, and these websites can also be good sources of information.

Air Plants: The Curious World of Tillandsias by Zenaida Sengo (Timber Press 2014)

Indoor Kitchen Gardening: Turn Your Home Into a Year-round Vegetable Garden by Millard Elizabeth (Cool Springs Press 2014)

Succulents Simplified: Growing, Designing, and Crafting with 100 Easy-Care Varieties by Debra Lee Baldwin (Timber Press, 2013)

The Pruning Book by Lee Reich (Taunton 2010)

What's Wrong With My Plant? (And How Do I Fix It?) by David Deardorff, Kathryn Wadsworth (Timber Press 2010)

In this series:
Plants from Pits by Holly Farrell (Mitchell Beazley 2015)

Red Hot Chili Grower by Kay Maguire (Mitchell Beazley 2015)

The Little Book of Bonsai by Malcolm and Kath Hughes (Mitchell Beazley 2016)

INDEX

CREDITS